THE MEANING
OF YOUR
DREAMS

(Formerly: What Your Dream Meant)

by
Franklin D. Martini

BELL PUBLISHING COMPANY · NEW YORK

TABLE OF CONTENTS

This book was written by the late Franklin D. Martini. He was an astrologist, palmist, handwriting analysist, and interpreter of dreams who wrote many books.

Great were his followers who believed and followed Martini's every word—spoken and written. In his day, his name was a familiar one in the homes of those who were believers of the occult sciences.

There were many people who put great faith in dreams. They believed these nocturnal visions forewarned good and evil, happiness and sadness, good luck and bad.

For these people, Martini wrote *The Meaning of Your Dreams*. He listed the most common dreams and gave them his interpretation. We have published his words, just as he wrote them, for the perusal and enjoyment of all.

The Publisher

A

"And the angel of God spoke to me in a dream, saying 'Jacob'; And I said, 'Here am I,'" *Gen.* xxxi., II.

ABCESS

To dream that you are suffering with such an affliction as the above, denotes that your misfortunes are likely to overwhelm you.

ABDOMEN

To dream that you see this part of your body, foretells that your greatest expectation will be realized, providing you redouble your energies on your labors instead of pleasure. Should you dream that this part of your body is sunken of shriveled, foretells that you will be persecuted by false friends.

To see it protruding, or swollen, signifies trials and tribulations, in which you may conquer by determination.

ABORTION

For a woman to dream that such an operation is being committed on her, is an indication that some scandal is hanging in her immediate future. For a physician to dream that he is interested in such an inhuman act, would foretell troubles to the dreamer brought about through lack of attention to his duties.

ABUSE

To dream of abusing an individual, foretells bad luck in your affairs. You are likely to lose money through the influence of others who may induce you to step against your will. To dream that someone abuses you, foretells that you will be molested in your daily affairs.

ACCIDENT

To dream of such a misfortune, is a warning to avoid any form of travel at least for the immediate time, as your life may be in danger.

ACHES

To dream of such symptoms foretells that you are too frank and open in your business dealings wherein others will profit by your ideas.

ACQUAINTANCE

To dream that you meet an acquaintance and the meeting results in a fuss or argument, it denotes a division in your family; in love, in fidelity, and perhaps losses in business.

ACTOR OR ACTRESS

To dream that you are in this profession, denotes that there is much hard work before you, but by persevering, your ambitions will be crowned. For a woman to dream that she is to marry an actor, denotes that her ambitions will be thwarted. For a man to dream that he is having a jolly good time with an actress (if married), family troubles (if single), friction with his sweatheart.

ADULTERY

To dream that you have perpetrated this act is in most cases a bad omen. Should the person be married of whom you dream, you can almost be sure that some trouble or misfortune is about to confront you. If she be a virgin, it would indicate an early invitation to a wedding. When a married woman dreams of adultery, it signifies that she will soon conceive, and is a strong sign that it will be a girl. If the woman be not married it would denote troubles and obstacles for her.

For a man to dream that he has had an opportunity to commit adultery and was unable to perpetrate the act through some physical inability, denotes a rival or competitor in business, sometimes an illness.

AFFLICTION

To dream that you see a friend suffering with an injury or affliction, denotes the receipt of money or good news.

AFRAID

To dream that you are afraid to go ahead with some project tells of discontent in your household, and business may suffer.

AGONY

To feel agony in your dreams is not a good sign, it tells of weariness and pleasure, the former is apt to predominate. To dream that you are in agony over monetary affairs is a sign that you will hear of the illness of some near friend.

AIR

To dream that you are inhaling hot air, is a sign that you will be influenced against your will. Cold air, denotes a falling off in business and in turn bringing family troubles.

ALLIGATOR

To dream that you see an alligator crawling, is a sign that you must exercise much care in any new step that you may contemplate.

ALMS HOUSE

To dream of this institution is indicative that one's marriage will not be a worldly one.

AMOROUS

To dream that you are possessed with such a sensation, would lead you towards some scandal.

ANGELS

To dream of these heavenly messengers, relaxes to a changed condition in the near future; it tells of good news and a possible legacy not a great distance hence.

ANTS

To dream of these little pests, foretells of many trifling annoyances in your daily doings that will tire you without accomplishing much of anything.

APES

To dream of apes in an omen of sickness and disease. To see one up a tree, the dreamer is warned to be careful of false and deceitful friends.

APPAREL

For a man to dream of womens apparel, denotes vexations, or temptations of some kind caused by a woman. If the apparel is of the gaudy order, illicit cohabitation may take place.

APPLES

To dream of apples is an excellent omen. To see them on trees; prosperity, (to eat them, if they be good and ripe), a signal for you to go ahead and carry out your plans.

APRON

To dream of an apron, foretells of an uneven course. For a woman to lose one, foretells censure and criticism from elders.

ARROWS

To dream that others are shooting arrows into your body, denotes that a pending suspicion will be verified.

ASCEND

To dream that you are ascending to some high point, but experience trouble in reaching it, foretells a disappointment.

ASSASSIN

To dream that you receive a blow from an assassin, you will be disappointed in your trials; to see blood, caused by the assassin in any form, is a sign of enemies endeavoring to destroy your conditions.

AUNT

To dream of your aunt is a sign that you will receive a calling down for an action you are not guilty of.

AUTOMOBILE

To dream that you are riding in an "auto," denotes that you will be restless and regret some deed or act.

B

"I believe it to be true that dreams are the true interpreters of our inclinations; but there is art required to sort and understand them."—Montaigue—*Essays*.

BABY

To dream that you hear a baby crying, is a sign of disappointment and sickness. To dream of a bright, healthy baby, denotes success in love and many warm friends. To dream of a sickly baby, tells of many trials.

BACHELOR

For a man to dream that he is reigning in the kingdom of bachelorhood, is a warning for the dreamer to keep clear from feminine genders, for the present at least, to keep on the safe side of the altar, as desperate designing women are lying in his wake.

BACON

To dream that you are eating bacon is considered good; rancid bacon tells of worries and trials.

BAKING

For a woman to dream of baking is not a good sign, it speaks of illness and the care of a large family, which may depend on her for support.

BALD

To dream that you see a man with a bald head, tells that enemies are trying to injure you in your interests, but by persevering you will outwit them.

BALLOON

For you to see in your dreams a balloon is a sign of slowness and falling off in business. To go up in one would mean an unpleasant journey.

BANANA

To dream of this fruit, denotes that you are likely to marry one with whom you will be unhappy—a mesalliance. To eat bananas, tell of a grind in business. To see them spoil, tells of an undertaking that will be distasteful to you.

BANJO

To dream of this instrument foretells a merry time for you in the near future. To see another playing a banjo, tells of slight worries which will soon fade away.

BANK

To see in your dream a bank without officers, is an omen of business losses. To see the tellers pay out money, tells of some careless act on your part. To receive from a bank is an omen of success.

BAR

To dream that you are behind a bar and mix drinks, denotes a desire to cover your action by deceptive plans.

BARBER

To dream of a man in this business, denotes that success will come to you after much hard work. For a woman to dream of a barber, is a sign that her fortune will come very slowly.

BASEBALL

To dream of baseball tells that you will cultivate contentment and become a cheerful companion. To dream that you are playing baseball, tells of much pleasure in the near future.

BATHING

To dream that you are bathing in clear water, is a sign of good fortune; to bath in warm water is generally a sign of some trouble; to go bathing with others, is an omen that you must be careful in the selection of your companions. To see people bathing, and if the water be perfectly clear that you can see the actions of their bodies, relates to honor and distinction. To dream that you are bathing yourself, foretells that you will confer a kindness to some person who will be very thankful.

BATS

It is a bad omen to dream of these noctural creatures, it foretells troubles, afflictions, even death is included.

BEANS

To dream of beans is not good. To see them grow is a sign of illness. Dried beans, means disappointment in material things. To eat them, signifies ill tidings from loved ones.

BEAR

To dream of this animal is a sign of great competition in pursuits of every description. To dream that you kill one is a sign that you will be able to release yourself from difficulties.

BEAUTY

To dream of beauty is an excellent omen. To dream of a beautiful woman is a sign of peace and plenty. It means success in business as well as in love.

BED

To dream that a bed is clean and neat, tells of ending worries. To dream that you are in a strange bed, is a sign of unexpected friends who are to visit you soon.

BEEF

To dream of beef that is raw, portends that bodily afflictions may attend you, also a sign of an injury, therefore it is advisable to keep your intellect with your senses. To eat beef, and it be tickling to the palate, means gains in business.

BEER

To drink beer; disappointments. To see others drink; some one will reveal a guilty intrigue of yours.

BEES

To dream of these busy little creatures, foretells a profitable undertaking. It would be well for the dreamer to act at once.

BEETLES

To see them crawling over you, denotes poor luck. To kill them is a good omen

BEGGAR

To dream of a beggar is a sign of poor business, generally caused by poor management. To give to a beggar, tells that you will soon be satisfied with your surroundings.

BELT

To dream that there is a belt around you, is a sign that you will meet a stranger who will create a good deal of gossip.

BET

To dream that you are betting on games of chances is a sign to be cautious in new undertakings. Evilminded competitors are trying to divert your attention into an illegitimate direction. Further, it is a sign that others are trying to wring money from you by some cunning device.

BIBLE

To dream of the holy book, denotes that some innocent act will be turned into some unexpected happiness.

BIRDS

It is a favorable omen to dream of birds, if their plumage is beautiful, a wealthy and happy partner will be yours. To see birds flying, denotes prosperity to the dreamer. To catch birds, is good to. To hear them speak, denotes a task near at hand which requires much caution. To kill them tells of misfortune.

BIRTH (Premature)

For a woman to dream that she gives birth to such as the above, denotes that the very next child will be bright and gain many credit marks from a scholarly standpoint. A childless woman to dream such will have her ambitions crowned with success.

BITE

To dream that something bites you, is a sign of much work ahead, also some indirect losses are threatened.

BLANKET

To dream of a blanket, if soiled, signifies treachery. If nice and clean, success and an illness averted through exercised caution.

BLEEDING

To dream that you are bleeding, tells of misfortune and possible death, and a possibility of many things to turn against you.

BLIND

To dream of blind people, foretells that some one will apply to you for financial aid. To dream you are afflicted in this manner, tells that a great change is to overtake you—probably from the height of success to the pit of poverty.

BLOOD

To dream that you see blood flowing from a wound, tells of physical ailment and much worry.

BLOSSOMS

To see in your dream, trees or like things in blossom, is a sign of peace and success in the near future.

BLUSHING

For you to dream that you are blushing, denotes that you will be greatly vexed over some false accusation. To see others blush, tells of some blunder caused by some awkward act of yours.

BONES

To dream of seeing a lot of bones, is a sign of bad influence about you.

BOOKS

To dream of studying them is a sign of honor and riches. To dream of old books, is a sign to keep away from evil. To dream of hunting for books; vexation.

BOOTS

To dream of old boots, indicates all illness and a displeasure. New boots, denotes luck in your dealings and an increase for your labors.

BOTTLES

To dream of bottles that are filled with some transparent fluid, is an elegant omen, it tells of prosperity in business and conquest in love.

BOX

To dream of opening a box, tells of riches and delightful journeys. If the box be empty; disappointment and crosses.

BRACELET

To dream that a bracelet is about your arm, perhaps the gift of a sweetheart, is a sign of an early marriage.

BREAD

To dream of seeing a lot of bread, is an omen of peace and plenty throughout life.

BRICK

To dream of a brick, foretells unsettled business and troubles in love.

BRIDE

For a young woman to dream that she is a bride, is a sign of money by inheritance, which will greatly delight the individual. To dream that you kiss a bride, shows a reunion between lovers.

BRIDGE

To dream that you cross a bridge safely, tells that you will overcome your obstacles and rapidly speed onward toward success. Should the bridge go down from under you, beware of false friends. To dream that you are crossing a bridge, even though it be bad, and are advised not to cross it, but get over it with ease, denotes good business. To dream of crossing a railroad bridge and there meet a train and are compelled to suspend your body from underneath, in order to save yourself, and do so with success, omens rewarded efforts in business.

BROOMS

To dream of brooms is a good sign, it tells of rapid strides towards success.

BROTHEL

To dream that you frequent a place of this kind, portends that your reputation is at stake through your material indulgences.

BRUSH

To dream of using a brush of any description, foretells that a mixed line of work will be assigned to you, yet withal you find pleasure and reward in doing it.

BUFFALO

To dream of buffalos is a sign of launching a large enterprise, in which you will be persevering, gain large profits.

BUGS

To dream of seeing bugs of some kind crawling out of your toilet articles, denotes an imminent illness to the dreamer. To dream that you crush a bug of some kind with your fingers, signifies that you will get a letter from a blood relative, telling you of dire straits and requests your aid financially. To dream that your head is literally covered with bugs and that they are inserting their heads into your scalp, denotes a disappointment pertaining to glory.

BUILDING

To dream that you are building, signifies that you will shortly meet with glory and distinction. To dream that you see a large building, denotes that you will shortly make a new acquaintance and will afterwards become intimate. To a lady, this dream means a new admirer.

BULL

To see one follow you, tells of trouble in business. To see one horning a person; bad luck may overtake you.

BURGLARS

To dream that they are rifling your pockets, denotes that you will have enemies to contend with.

To see you home or place of business ransacked by these intruders, is a sign that your good name will be assailed. Here your courage should defend you.

BURN

To dream that you are burning yourself is a good sign, it denotes that your ambition will be crowned and much good health is yours.

BUSINESS

To dream that you are going into business, but are disappointed in receiving your goods and fixtures, denotes a disappointment of a letter containing important news.

To dream that you are seeking a location to open a place of business and are unable to find a location, having already bought your goods, and upon returning you lose all your goods by storm, signifies a loss of personal property.

To dream that some one is trying to put you out of business, denotes that you have been cheated in some purchase.

BUTTER

To dream that you are eating fresh butter, denotes that your plans will be successfully carried out and be richly rewarded. To eat rancid butter speaks of many struggles relating to manual labor.

BUTTERFLY

To dream of a butterfly is a sign of happiness, success and much popularity.

BUTTONS

For a young woman to dream that she is sewing on buttons, denotes that she is soon to meet a wealthy man who will become her partner in marriage. To a youth it signifies honor and wealth.

C

And yet as angels in some brighter dreams
Call it the soul when man doth sleep.
So some strange thoughts transcend our wonted dreams
And into glory peep.—VAUGHN.—*Ascension Hymn.*

CABBAGE

To dream of cabbage is as a rule not good. It portends toward trouble in many forms. Should you see it green it would mean troubles in love and unfaithfulness in marriage. To dream that you gather cabbage would denote that your extravagance might bring you to want.

CAGE

To dream of a cage and if there is a bird within, implies that much wealth and many splendid things are coming your way. It is also a sign of a wealthy marriage. To dream of a cage that has animals within, and if the animals appear tame and peaceful, you will triumph over your enemies.

CAKE WALK

To dream that you see people do the cake walk, or similar grostesque movements, implies that you will receive news from an old friend telling the doings of others that you know.

CAKES

To dream of cakes is a propitious omen. A large and lucious looking cake would denote much success in some new enterprise. Also much pleasure from both society and business.

CALVES

To dream of a peaceful calf grazing on the hills, foretells of much joy and many pleasant associates, and a sign of early good fortune.

CAMERA

To dream of this photograph instrument, signifies that changes may bring about unpleasant results. To dream that you are taking pictures, denotes that something will occur that will be very displeasing to you.

CANARY BIRDS

To dream of these singers, portends of unexpected joy. To dream that you own a canary bird, foretells that you will acquire much honor and distinction.

CANDLES

To dream that you see candles burn, denotes that a nice little fortune will be yours some day. To a woman, it tells that a splendid offer of marriage is approaching her, which she should not hesitate to accept.

CANDY

To dream that you are eating candy and it is pleasing to the nerves of the palate, denotes that you will have some money refunded that had been paid.

CANE

To see a field of cane in your dream, is a sign of advancement in your business in the near future.

CANOE

To dream that you are canoeing on a perfectly calm stream, tells that you believe in your abilities and are a born leader, consequently should strike out for yourself. To dream that you are on rough water would mean much trouble in the beginning of any business venture.

CAP

To dream of seeing a cap always relates to some public work, perhaps to take part in some festivity. To dream of losing a cap would mean that your courage would fail you in time of danger.

CARPENTER

To dream that you see these mechanics at their work, portends success to you, acquired in a legitimate way, and little danger of losing your all.

CARPET

To dream of carpet, and if the color be fresh and pleasing to the eye, denotes much wealth and many true friends. To dream that you are laying carpet, you will have cause to go on a pleasant journey, also a profitable one.

CARS

To dream of cars always refers to journeys, and many changes. To dream that you have missed your car and are much wrought up over it, denotes that you will be foiled in your plan of promoting your business.

CARVING

To dream that you are carving a roast or a fowl, is not an omen of great worldly success, as others may constantly hamper you in your efforts. To dream of carving meat of any kind, and your present business is poor, it would be advisable to change or conceive new methods to improve your present condition.

CASH

To dream that you have an abundance of cash, but it is not yours, denotes that your friends look upon you as mercenary and unfeeling. To dream that you spend borrowed money, tells that you will be discovered in your deceptive effusive kindliness.

CASKET

To dream that you see a casket and remove the lid of the same, denotes that you will soon buy flowers to adorn the casket of a relative or friend.

CASTOR OIL

To dream of this oil, denotes that you are accusing a friend upon the hearsay of another, which is unjust.

CATERPILLAR

To dream of a catepillar, denotes a tendency of being placed into embarrassing situations, and little chance for progress. It also speaks of deceptive friends. You would do well in being cautious to whom you speak.

CATS

To dream that a vicious cat attacks you and you are unable to drive it away, foretells that you have desperate enemies who will make it a point to blacken your reputation and cause the loss of property through fire, from which legal difficulties may arise. If you are able to scare the cat away you will overcome great obstacles. To dream of a cat that appears tame and gentle, speaks of deceptive friends who may not injure you or harm you, but annoy in matters pertaining to gossiping.

CELERY

To dream of celery is a propitious omen. It speaks of prosperity and power beyond your wildest hopes. To eat it, unlimited love and affection will be showered upon you.

CELLAR

To dream of a cellar is often a sign of approaching illness, also that you may lose confidence in your associate, and thereby lose property. For a young woman to dream of a cellar denotes an offer of marriage from a gambler.

CEMETERY

To dream of a well arranged and well kept cemetery, denotes prosperity and that you will regain property that you had figured as lost, or perhaps hear of friends that you have mourned as dead.

CESSPOOL

To dream that a sink or cesspool is overflowing and its contents go in all directions, denotes that stormy elements may destroy personal property.

CHAINS

To dream of breaking a chain, denotes torment and difficulties, to see another bound in chains, a loss of money or an unpleasant business engagement.

CHAIR

To dream of a chair, portends that you will fail to keep some important obligation. To see another sitting in a chair, speaks of some bad tidings.

CHEATED

To dream that some one has cheated you in a deal, denotes that you will meet designing people, who will endeavor to wrest from you, part of your fortune. For the young to dream of being cheated, tells of quarrels and troubles in love.

CHEESE

To dream of eating cheese, speaks of sorrows and difficulties. To make it; profit and gain.

CHERRIES

To dream of picking cherries out of season, denotes an annoyance from an enemy or former friend. To dream that you eat a dried cherry and find that the pit resembles that of a diamond, signifies that you will hear of a bitter disappointment.

CHESTNUTS

To dream that you find chestnuts and eat them, denotes success in love, or that you will meet with some pleasant experience with the opposite sex. To eat boiled chestnuts, implies that you will have success in business. To dream you prick your hands with the burr, shows that you will be deceived by a pretended friend.

CHICKENS

For you to dream of a brood of chickens, tells of many cares and petty worries, some of which will ultimately turn to your benefit. Young chickens are good to dream of if you are contemplating some venture.

CHILD

To dream of children is a splendid augury. If a woman dreams of giving birth to a child, it denotes a legacy or other good fortune. If she be a maid and dreaming the above, she should exercise much care or she will lose her virtue. To dream that you see a child dropping from a boat into water, and then being rescued safely, stands for good news.

CHILDREN

To dream of seeing several children about the house is good, and if the dreamer in reality has none, is portentous of success and many blessings. To dream of seeing your child ill or dead, it is well for the dreamer to exercise much care and good judgment, as the child's welfare may be threatened. To dream of a dead child, implies that troubles are at hand. To dream of playing with children, denotes that much happiness is in store for you.

CHINA

For a woman to dream of cleaning or arranging her treasured pieces of china, denotes that she will be domestic and home loving in her views and will help to require much of this world's goods.

CHOCOLATE

To dream of drinking chocolate, denotes that you will prosper after you have conquered your little difficulties. To see chocolate, tells that you will provide plenty for those who are looking to you for support.

CHRIST

To dream of Christ, denotes contentment and that you are greatly beloved by your fellowmen, highly esteemed and many gains brought about by the prestage and influence of others.

CHRISTMAS TREE

To dream of this tree, tells of good fortunes and many joyful occasions.

CHURCH

To dream of entering one, denotes benevolence and honorable conduct. To pray in one; joy and consolation. Should you enter in gloom, you will soon attend a funeral.

CIDER

To dream that you drink cider, denotes a dispute and that you are confiding in friends who are not worthy of your confidence.

CISTERN

To dream that you fall into one, denotes troubles, caused through the trespassing upon the rights and pleasures of others.

CITY

To dream that you are in a strange city, or lost in a city, denotes that you will soon change your residence or place of abode.

CLAIRVOYANT

To dream of being possessed with this psychic power, speaks of a possibility of changing your present occupation, which may arouse much enmity with your new associates and thereby making it unpleasant for you. To dream of consulting one, implies of friction in your family affairs.

CLIMB

To dream that you are climbing and reach the desired spot, denotes glory and distinction for you.

CLOCK

To dream of a clock, denotes trouble from a backbiter; to hear it strike, some bad news, perhaps that of an illness, or the death of a near friend.

CLOTHES

To dream of seeing old and soiled clothing, denotes that a conspiracy is under way to harm you.

Be cautious when dealing with friendly strangers. For a woman to dream that her clothes are soiled or torn, there is danger of some one talking ill of her character. To dream of clean and new clothes, is an excellent omen. To dream that you have a very large wardrobe, in fact so many clothes that you don't know what to do with them, is a sign that you may come to want for necessaries of life. Sometimes legal difficulties are threatened.

CLOUDS

To dream that a clouded canopy is over-hanging the earth, implies to ill luck on account of bad management. Should they turn into rain it is por-tentuous of troubles caused from sickness. To dream that you see bright clouds, denotes that happiness will be yours, after the clouds have passed away.

CLOWN

To dream of seeing a clown going through his grotesque movements, denotes some vexations and annoyances from near associates.

COACH

To dream that you are running a coach and the same is full of people, signifies that you will be greatly surprised by the meeting or visiting of a friend or near relative.

COALS

To dream of seeing red-hot coals, portends a pleasant change and many pleasures.

COCK-CROWING

To hear in your dreams the crowing of a cock in the early morn, is a propitious indication. To a single person it foretells an early marriage, and all the comforts of home. To dream of seeing cocks fight, would foretell of disaster in your family affairs that may lead to separation.

COCKTAIL

To dream that you are drinking cocktails, denotes that you will have troubles with your friends through a fault of your own. Perhaps through jealously that you may arouse by not treating them all alike.

COFFEE

To dream that you are drinking it, if you be single, is a sign that you will have oppositions as regarding marriage. If married, possible family trouble that can be avoided by proper care.

COFFIN

To dream of a coffin is an unpropitious omen. It means unavoidable losses to a man in business. To dream of seeing your coffin, much unpleasantness from the opposite sex.

COINS

To dream of gold coins, portends of much success, consequently may see many of the great wonders of the world. To dream of silver coins is not so fortunate, they usually bring about strife and contention.

COMEDY

For you to be at play of this kind in your dreams, is a sign that you will waste much time by indulging in short-lived pleasures.

COMPANION

To dream of seeing an old companion, may bring about anxieties and perhaps temporary illness.

COMPOSING

To dream that you are engaged in composing, denotes that some difficulties will arise, which will require a great effort on your part to solve them.

CONCUBINE

For a man to dream that he is in company with a woman of this character, is an indication that he is in great danger of public disgrace; his dual life will be brought to light. For a woman to dream that she is a woman of this type, denotes that she has little selfrespect and cares little for public opinion.

COOKING

To dream that you are cooking, implies that you will be called upon to perform some pleasant duties. Friends will visit whom you thought had no regard for you.

COPYING

To dream that you are copying, portends to an unfavorable working of a plan of which you thought very favorable.

CORN

To dream of corn is a good omen, it speaks of many pleasures and a successful career. To dream that you helped to gather a large heap of corn, is an indication that you will rejoice in the prosperity of some friend.

CORNS

To dream that your corns are painful, denotes that enemies are endeavoring to injure you. Should you dream that you succeeded in getting rid of your corns, is indicative that you may inherit a legacy from some unknown source.

CORPSE

To dream that you see a corpse lying in a coffin, foretells that you will receive sad news, perhaps the illness of a friend, usually the opposite sex. To dream of a lot of corpses lying in state, yet nothing distressing about them, is an augury of great success, in some cases an apology from one who has deeply wronged you in the past.

CORSET

To dream that you have much difficulties in the undoing of your corset, portends that you will have some quarrel with a friend upon the slightest cause.

COUCH

To dream of lounging on a couch, denotes that you are laboring under a false impression regarding some happening. Think twice before you speak.

COUNTING

To dream of counting some object is propitious, it denotes a fair sailing and that you are perfectly able to meet your obligations. Should you dream of counting out an object, such as money, to another, is a sign of losses. To count for yourself is good, to count out is bad.

COWS

To dream of cows is a good omen, it foretells of an abundance throughout life, particularly in the line of viands.

CRABS

To dream of seeing crabs crawl, denotes that you will be compelled to solve many complicated affairs. The dreamer may have rivals (if single) in love affairs.

CREAM

To dream of cream in any form, or quality is an excellent omen, it denotes that you will be associated with riches and have a bright future before you.

CRICKET

To dream that you hear the noise of a cricket, is an unpleasant indication, it portends towards serious news, perhaps bereavement.

CRIMINAL

To dream that you see the escape of a criminal who has committed a crime, denotes that you will be annoyed by friends who desire your influence for their own person gain. To dream of apprehending a criminal, foretells that you will come into the possession of secrets that may jeopardize your freedom.

CRIPPLE

To see in your dream an unfortunate cripple, denotes that you will be appealed to for alms by an old associate. In which it would be safe for you to give a helping hand, as some day you will be rewarded for your kindness.

CROSS

To dream of a cross, implies that there is immediate trouble ahead, so prepare for difficulties.

CROW

To see crows in your dream, portends to unpleasant tidings. To hear them caw, others may influence you against your better judgment in some business proposition.

CRUTCHES

To dream that you are compelled to use them, denotes that you are too dependent and lack self-reliance, consequently no power to spur ahead.

CRYING

To dream that some near friend comes to you crying and seemingly in deep distress, denotes that you will learn of some loss, either by fire or water in which you may not be interested financially, but from a sympathetic standpoint. To a working individual this dream may denote a loss of position.

CRYING

To dream that you are crying, denotes that some happy affair will subside into gloom. To see others crying, implies that you will learn the financial distress of some near relative, which is pitiful to behold.

CUT

To dream of a cut, denotes a possible illness, or the evil doings of supposed friends may disturb your cheerfulness.

D

Dreams in their development have breath,
And tears, and tortures, and the touch of joy,
They have a weight upon our working thought,
They take a weight from off our waking toils,
They do divide our being.—BYRON.—*The Dream.*

DAGGER

To see this weapon in your dream, speaks of enemies. If you succeed in getting it away from your assailant, you will conquer your enemies.

DANCING

To dream of dancing, signifies much pleasure and a possible inheritance.

DANDELION

To dream of this common green, implies health, happiness and success.

DARKNESS

To dream that you are on a journey and darkness overtakes you, generally speaks of poor success in the thing you are about to attempt.

DEATH

To dream that you see some one dying amid agony, foretells that you will shed tears before the day is over, out of pure sympathy for another.

DEBT

To dream that you have a debt, and are unable to meet your obligations, foretells a worry in business or love.

DEER

To dream of this animal is a good omen, it speaks of deep and sincere friendship to the unmarried and much happiness to the married. To kill one is a sign that you will be bound and goaded by your backbiters.

DENTIST

To dream that you are having some dental work done, is a sign that some supposed friend is not worthy of your confidence, you are likely to be betrayed.

DESERT

To dream that you are wandering through arid land, denotes loss of property and possible life.

DESTRUCTION

To dream that your requisites to do business with, suffer destruction, portends that you will miss a lot of business by entertaining company.

DETECTIVE

To dream of this officer, and that he has a charge against you of which you are innocent, implies that success is drawing nearer you each day. To dream that you are guilty, denotes that you will lose your reputation and that friends will turn against you.

DEVIL

To dream of "His Santanic Majesty," is never a good omen, it speaks of bad influences working against you; deceitful friends, etc.

DIAMONDS

To dream that you wear diamonds, is a sign that you will be crossed in love, or that your lover is not true. For a man to dream of this precious stone, or that he is dealing in them is a sure sign that he will become rich and gain high position in life. To dream of diamonds is usually propitious, unless you dream that you have stolen them.

DIGGING

To dream of digging into the earth, implies that you will never come to want, but life may be a laborious one. Should you dream of finding some precious metal while digging, would speak of a favorable turn in your fortune. Should the ground slide back into the hole, or the hole become filled with water, would imply that in spite of the most strenuous efforts, things will not come your way.

DISEASE

To see in your dream a sucerer from a venereal disease, contracted by an illicit attachment, foretells bad tidings from an enemy who is trying to defame you to a near friend. To dream of diseases in general, augurs luck and success also this dream goes by contrary.

DIVING

To dream of diving into water that is clear, denotes a favorable ending of some unpleasant ordeal. If it be muddy, things will go from bad to worse.

DIVORCE

To dream of severing the connubial knot, is a sign that you are not happy with your companion and should strive to study one another and avoid noting faults, or the matrimonial bark may strike the rock of discontent.

DOCTOR

To dream of a doctor, is a propitious omen, denoting prosperity and good health, particularly so if he calls socially, for you will then not have cause to spend your money for his services. To dream that you send for a doctor because you are ill, may portend to some friction in the family. To dream that he does some cutting but no blood is seen, foretells that you will be annoyed by some person who tries to extort money from you.

DOGS

To dream of a vicious dog, yet succeeding in warding him off, implies that you will conquer your enemies. To dream that a dog is giving birth to puppies; a disappointment over which you are ruffled, will turn out to your advantage in the end. To dream of dogs, is as a rule good; but if the dog snarls or barks at you, it foretells quarrels relating to business and that jealous enemies are endeavoring to destroy your happiness and reputation,

DOVES

To dream of doves, denotes happiness and peace, and that harmony will reign supreme in your family, it is a sign that you will be blessed with happy and obedient children.

DRAMA

To dream that you witness a drama, relates to pleasant meetings with some distant friends. Should the drama fail to be interesting to you, it foretells that you will be forced to associate with unpleasant companions.

DRESS

To dream that you find a woman's dress, or wearing apparel in your wardrobe, signifies troubles and vexations, caused by a woman, usually at a very delicate moment that proves very exasperating.

DRINKING

To dream that you are going into a public place to take a drink, and there see acquaintances whom you invite; they accepting your offer, and friendship seems to prevail throughout, implies that you will make a speculation, or embark in a new business.

Should a party refuse your invitation, the one in question being a relative, denotes that you will meet an old-time acquaintance and have a long chat.

DRIVING

To dream that you are out driving with family or relatives, and you come across unpleasant roads, denotes some unfortunate happening. To dream that you are out driving with a woman, is a sure disappointment. To dream that you are out driving with men, foretells a gain, or success in business. To dream that the horses give out from exhaustion, or that you come to a place that you are unable to cross, denotes some bad news relating to business.

DROWNING

To dream that you see another drowning, or that you are drowning yourself, denotes much good to the dreamer. To the lover, an early marriage. To a girl, it will be well for her to keep an eye on her sweetheart.

DUCKS

To dream of these fowls, denotes a surprise by a friend, who may call and dine with you. To see them killed, speaks of enemies who may interfere with your doings. To see them flying, foretells a change in business for the better. To hunt them, a possible difficulty with your employer.

DUST

To dream that you are covered with dust, is a sign that you may have some losses in business through the failure of others. This would hold particularly true if it should rain on you while you are covered with dust.

DYEING

To dream that you are dyeing, is a sign that some evil is lying in your wake that may arrest your progress in your efforts, at least for the time being.

E

"Is this a dream? O! if it be a dream.
Let me sleep on, and do not wake me yet."—
LONGFELLOW.—*Spanish Student.*

EAGLES

To dream that you see an eagle soaring above you, foretells lofty ambition, for which you will encounter great difficulty in realizing, nevertheless you will gain your desires by perservering. Should you dream of killing an eagle, would signify that you will associate with people in high standing who will bring you much influence regarding position and power in life. To dream that you ride on an eagle's back, foretells that you will take a long journey, very likely into a foreign country.

EARRINGS

To dream of earrings, is an omen that you will have much encouraging and interesting work to do.

EATING

To dream that you are eating alone, is an indication of losses and depressed spirits. To eat with others or in company, denotes success, happy environments and undertakings that will be profitable.

EEL

To dream of an eel and that you are able to hold on to it, is propitious. To dream that one got away from you, denotes that your business may suffer. To see one in clear water is also good.

EGGS

To dream that you find a nest of eggs, is an excellent sign, it augurs happiness and contentment; also a sign of many and healthy children, a happy love affair to the unmarried. To dream of rotten eggs, speaks of troubles and losses. To dream of birds egg and that you crawled up a tree after them, denotes that you will gain money very unexpected.

ELECTRICITY

To dream of this mysterious force, denotes some immediate offer which will afford you much pleasure and success. Should you receive a shock, a danger may lie in your path. To see in your dream a live wire, denotes that designing enemies are endeavoring to overthrow your plans.

ELEPHANT

To dream that you see one of of these monsters of the forest, is a happy augury, it tells of peace and plenty. To dream of many, you will gain fame in the art of riches. To feed one, denotes a change in your work shortly.

ELOPEMENT

To dream of such romance is unfavorable. To married people, it shows that they are holding a position that they are unworthy of, and chances are that they may have trouble in the same. To unmarried ones, it tells of much trouble in love affairs.

EMPLOYMENT

To dream that you are seeking employment, is good, it denotes that you are very energetic, full of force; your services appreciated, and will have little cause to seek work. Should you be out of work, and dream that you have work, would denote, if you are a wage earner, that you may be laid off for a short period, due to slack business.

ENEMIES

To dream that you meet an enemy and you endeavor to apologize for some wrong committed; but the enemy ignores the apology, foretells a business disappointment. To dream that you overcome your enemies, is a sign that you will succeed in your business and become rich. To conquer an enemy, is a happy augury.

ENGINE

To dream of this iron steed, would foretell unpleasant journeys, but turning out good after reaching your destination. To dream that you see an engine wrecked, would portend towards losses.

ENGRAVING

To dream that you are engaged in engraving, but through lack of ability, are unable to finish the job, foretells of a disappointment to a friend, whom you are eagerly awaiting to meet.

ENTERTAINMENT

To dream that you are a patron at an entertainment, where there is music that pleases your fancy, denotes good tidings from friends that are absent.

ESCAPE

To dream that you escape from imprisonment, or a cloistered life, implies that you will have rapid rises in the business world. To dream that you make an attempt, and are caught in the act, speaks of unpleasant notoriety to fall on you.

EXECUTION

To dream that you witness an execution, signifies that you will suffer some loss, due to the doings of others. Should you dream that you are to be executed, but some one will come to the rescue and save you, denotes that you will succeed in overcoming your enemies.

EXCREMENT

To dream of effete matter, denotes a change in your social surroundings.

EYEGLASS

To dream of finding an eyeglass, portends that you have friends, whom you do not care for, yet do not wish to offend them by telling them so.

EYES

To dream of seeing eyes staring at you with a hard and calculating expression, warns you to be cautious of enemies who are trying to injure you. For lovers to dream of eyes, denotes that they will have rivals that may be victorious. To dream of losing an eye, is an indication of illness.

F

"There are more things in Heaven and Earth than are dreamt of in your philosophy, Horatio"— *Shakespeare.*

FACE

To dream that you see a face is a happy omen, providing it is pleasant and cheerful. A frowning face, or one, distorted, would be significant of trouble.

FAECES

To dream that you are relinquishing waste matter, of faeces, denotes a disappointment in money matters, which may inconvenience you very much.

FAINTING

To dream that you are fainting, is a sign of a possible illness, also distressing news from the absent. To dream of seeing others faint is a sign of good news.

FALL

To dream that you are falling from a high place, and are much frightened in the flight, but sustain no injuries, denotes that you will overcome some obstacle that is hindering you now. To suffer injuries would signify obstacles that would go from bad to worse.

FAME

To dream that you have acquired fame, implies that you are following a mistaken ambition. To dream of others who have made their mark in the world, denotes that you will rise from obscurity to the top rung of the ladder of fame.

FAN

To dream of using or seeing a fan, portends that good news is awaiting you. It is also an omen of reviving an old friendship that may end very profitable.

FAT

To dream that you are growing very fat, tells that you will soon change from your present place, which will be good. To see others is also good.

FATIGUE

To dream that you are very fatigued, denotes a run down vitality, which is open to disease. In business things will diminish in power.

FEARS

To dream that you feel nervous and fearful over some matter, augurs that your prospective plans may come to naught. For the unmarried to dream such, denotes disappointment.

FEATHERS

To dream that you see many feathers about you, is an omen that your ambition will be crowned, and that you will rise to great height in power. To dream of ornamental feathers, augurs that you will become very popular socially.

FEET

To dream that your feet are hurting you, is an indication of much vexation, and troubles may creep into the family.

FEVER

To dream that you have been taken with a fever, denotes that you are too apprehensive and are wearing down your nerves by useless anxiety. Live in the "Now," and go in to win. Don't spoil to-day by yesterday. To dream of others being sick, denotes that some one in the family may soon suffer with illness.

FIGHT

If you dream that you are engaged in fight, it foretells to a man of business that he will soon make a change that will prove successful; to a laboring man, it predicts a raise in wages. To see others fighting, denotes carelessness in the spending of money and time. To dream that you whip your assailant, implies that you will win honor and wealth in spite of opposition.

FIGURING

To dream that you are figuring up a large column or doing an example that you find very difficult, denotes to the dreamer that he must be very cautious in the expressions regarding a business deal, for fear he may fail to influence the party concerned.

FINGERS

To dream of this part of your hand, generally speaks of a gain. For you to dream that they are cut or hurt, would imply much hard work throughout life. To dream that you have lost your fingers, is an omen of legal difficulties over money matters.

FIRE

To dream that you see something on fire and succeed in extinguishing the blaze before it gains much headway, denotes that you will be surprised very unexpectedly. To dream of fire, is a happy augury, so long as you do not get burned. To dream that your place of business is in ruins, denotes that you will become very much discouraged as regarding your business, but some unforseen good fortune will bear you up and give you new hope.

FIREWORKS

To dream of witnessing a grand display of fireworks, is a happy augur of much good health and enjoyment.

FISH

To dream of seeing fish swimming in clear water is very good, it's an omen that you will be favored by the rich and powerful.

FISHING

To dream of fishing in clear water, and can see the fish bite and are successful in catching them, denotes to the dreamer that he will discover something greatly to his advantage, which may bring forth riches. But if you fail to catch any, your efforts to obtain wealth will be difficult.

FITS

To dream of being afflicted with such, is indicative of an illness, thereby unable to attend to your duties. To dream of seeing others suffering from such, is a sign of much underhandedness among your fellow workers.

FLAG

To dream of your country's flag, relates to much success and victory. For the unmarried to dream of their flag, portends to admiration from a soldier.

FLEAS

To dream of these little pests, indicates irritation from close associates, which may cause you to exhibit your temper.

FLIES

To dream that you see an unlimited amount of flies about you, denotes that you are in danger of being threatened with an illness, also that enemies are endeavoring to destroy your efforts.

FLOOD

To dream that you are in a flood and the waters rise and recede gently and besides being clear, denotes peace and plenty. To dream of floods destroying much property, besides the water being muddy, speaks of sickness, troubles and losses, and much unhappiness in family affairs.

FLOWERS

To see in your dream many flowers, denotes pleasure and gains. For a young woman to dream of receiving flowers, is a sign that she will have many suitors. To dream of withered flowers, augurs a disappointment.

FLOWERS (Artificial)

To dream that you see some one make artificial flowers, signifies that you will be astonished at an exorbitant price charged by some one who renders you a service.

FLYING

To dream that you are flying, is a very good omen, providing you fly low, it tells a rise in the near future by falling into a higher position, and thereby made happy. To the lover, it is a sign that your sweetheart is true to you. To fly over clear water, is an omen of much marital happiness.

FOREST

To dream of being lost in one, signifies profit to the poor and loss to the rich.

FORTUNE-TELLER

To dream that you are consulting a fortune-teller, implies that you are undecided regarding some important matter. In case of this kind it is well to "trust the current that knows its way" and obey your first impression.

FOUNTAIN

To dream of seeing a fountain playing in the sunlight speaks of pleasant journeys and vast possessions.

FOX

To dream of a sly fox, is an indication of thieves annoying you; to fight with one speaks of an enemy who is crafty and subtle. To dream of a tame fox is good, it denotes that your affections will not be betrayed.

FRIENDS

To dream of friends being well and prosperous, denotes that you may soon see them and enjoy a merry time.

FROGS

To dream of seeing frogs hop about, denotes that you will have many sincere friends as your associates. To dream of catching them, is often a prognostic of a rundown vitality.

FRUITS

To dream of fruit out of season, denotes struggles and unpleasant things to contend with; in season it is always good, if it be ripe, very good.

FUNERAL

To dream of a funeral of a relative or friend, augurs riches, happiness, legacies, brilliant marriage. To dream of the funeral of a stranger, speaks of scandal and deep underhand practices.

G

"There is some ill a-brewing toward my rest, for I did dream of money bags to-night."—Shakespeare—*Merchant of Venice.*

GALLOWS

To dream of seeing another on the gallows of execution, implies that much care must be exercised in order to avoid pending danger. To dream that you are hanging yourself on a similar construction, indicates that friends are endeavoring to malign you.

GAMBLING

To dream that you are gambling and win much money, denotes a loss of friends. To lose; consolation, relief from troubles.

GAS

To dream that you are overcome by gas, denotes that you will have trouble, due to your own carelessness.

GEESE

To dream that you see geese or hear the quacking, implies that you will soon rise from your present circumstances. Very good, if you see them swimming in clear water.

GEMS

To dream of valuable gems, denotes that a happy fate is before you, both in love and business.

GHOSTS

To dream of the spirit of one dead, and if clad in white with a cheerful expression, denotes consolation and happiness; to see one with a revolting expression; temptation from alluring wiles from the opposite sex. For a ghost to speak to you, implies that you will be decoyed into the hands of evil doers.

GIFT

To dream that you have received a gift is a splendid omen, it denotes that you have no difficulties in meeting your payments, it is also an excellent indication in speculation and in affairs of the heart. To send a gift, would mean that displeasure would be cast your way. To dream that you receive one from an unmarried lady, tells of friendship. From a married lady, illicit proposals.

GIRLS

To dream of seeing a lot of girls, foretells encouraging prospects and many joys. For a man to dream that he is a girl, is a warning for him to be careful or his sexual desires may lead him to become a perversionist.

GLASS

To dream that you are looking into a glass or mirror, refers to trouble in your family affairs. To dream that some one gives you a glass and you let it fall, denotes that quarrels are near at hand.

GLOOMY

To dream that you feel gloomy and discouraged, denotes that you will soon hear of very discouraging news.

GLOVES

To dream that you have gloves on your hands, denotes honor, pleasure and prosperity. To dream that you lost your gloves, tells that you will shortly have a quarrel with a loved one. To dream of wearing an old pair of gloves of which you have been ashamed, tells that you will be betrayed and may thereby suffer a loss.

GOLD

To dream that you find gold, is an omen of honors and riches; to spend it, sorrow and disappointment. To dream of hiding gold, denotes that you will revenge yourself for some petty deed. To dream that you have a gold mine, denotes that you will become avaricious and mercenary.

GOSSIP

To dream that you have been gossiping about an affair that you had no right to, denotes that you will undergo an annoying anxiety. To dream that others have been gossiping about you is good, you will have some very pleasant surprise.

GRAMMAR

To dream that you are studying this book of language, implies that you will soon make some wise venture that will prove very profitable.

GRAPES

To dream that you see grapes in abundance, besides eating some, is a good omen. If they were pleasing to the taste, many pleasures and successes are before you; if they be sour and unpleasant to the taste, would foretell sorrow and trouble. For a maiden to dream of eating grapes, is an omen that she will soon marry; to pick grapes only, denotes that you will meet a stranger.

GRAVE

To dream of a grave, is not a good omen. To look into an empty grave, portends toward unpleasant tidings, generally relating to losses. To dream of digging a grave, denotes that others are endeavoring to thwart you in your efforts. To see your own grave, also speaks of enemies that are seeking to wrong you.

GREASE

To dream that grease is about your body, or on your clothes, signifies that plans you had figured on being profitable may slip from under you and amount to nothing.

GROCERIES

To dream that you have bought a lot of groceries, if they be fresh, is an excellent omen, it denotes peace and plenty.

GUITAR

To dream that you hear soft strains from a guitar, denotes to the dreamer that he must fortify himself against the clever wiles of seductive women. For a young woman to dream of hearing music from a guitar, denotes interferences in her closest affections. To play on this instrument, augurs happy family affairs.

GULLS

To dream of these water scavengers is an omen that possessions will rapidly increase in value.

GUN

To dream of hearing the sound of one, denotes trouble in your work. To dream of shooting with one, would imply a misfortune. To dream of this weapon is always a bad omen, whether you see it, or use it.

GYPSY

To dream of this wondering tribe denotes that your immediate future is hanging to uncertainties. For a woman to dream that a gypsy is reading her hand, is a sign of an early but unwise marriage. For a man to dream of consulting one, would tell that he is in danger of losing some valuable belongings.

H

"We are such stuff as dreams are made of, and our life is rounded with a sleep."—Shakespeare—*Tempest.*

HAIL

To dream that you are caught in a hail storm, denotes poor success in your prospective venture. To watch hail falling, portends to trouble and sadness.

HAIR

For a woman to dream that she has beautiful hair, and in reality has not, denotes carelessness of her personality, also poor mental power through lack of development. For a man to dream that he is losing his hair, denotes that he may become poor through his overly generous habits. To dream that you had your hair cut close to the head, denotes that your willful waste will bring you to woeful want. For a man to dream of having hair as long as that of a woman, denotes effeminacy and weakness of character. To dream of seeing a woman bald, denotes poverty and sickness. For a woman to dream that her hair is turning gray, and if she be unmarried, foretells that she will experience great difficulty in deciding which one of her lovers to choose as a husband.

HAND

To dream of having beautiful and well-groomed hands, denotes that you will rapidly rise in your calling and reach distinction. To dream that they are ugly or malformed, speaks of disappointments and hard times. To see blood on your hands, denotes quarrels and contention in your family. To dream that your hands are tied, tells of troubles in business.

HANDCUFFS

To dream of having these bracelets about your wrist, denotes that you will be greatly vexed by enemies. To succeed in releasing yourself from them, denotes that you will escape the plans designed for you by your enemies.

HAREM

To dream that you are the keeper of a harem, implies that you are scattering your best efforts on base pleasures. For a woman to dream that she is an inmate of such, denotes that she may resort to unlawful pleasures, or bask in the smiles of married men.

HARLOT

To dream of being in company with a woman of this character, denotes an over-indulgence in pleasures that may terminate disastrously. To dream of marrying one, would mean many hard and unpleasant things to face the rest of your life.

HARVESTER

To see many of them at work, denotes prosperity; to see them in repose, poor success in the near future.

HAT

To dream of wearing a soiled hat, predicts damage and dishonor. To dream of wearing a new hat, denotes a change of home and business, which will turn out prosperous. To lose your hat, implies that you will be vexed over some business affairs.

HATCHET

To dream of a hatchet, is a warning to expect peril or death. If it is broken or rusty, you will have troubles over disobedient people.

HAWK

To dream of a hawk, foretells that you are apt to be cheated by one in whom you had the utmost confidence. To succeed in shooting one, implies that you will by persevering surmount all obstacles. To shoot at a hawk and miss it, denotes enemies, who are endeavoring to malign you.

HAY

To dream that you see hay, denotes that you will have the honor to be invited to a merry-making. You will also render your service to some distinguished personage. To dream that you are hauling and putting hay into your barn, augurs a very good fortune, and that you will realize much profit from some enterprise.

HEAD

To dream of seeing a head severed from the body, and fresh blood about it, speaks of very bitter disappointments. To dream of seeing yourself with more than one head, denotes a sudden change for the better in your occupation. To dream of the head of a savage beast, denotes that your desires run on a low plane, and are given greatly to material pleasures, in fact, ruled by the animal world.

HEARSE

To dream of a hearse, implies that an illness may enter your home in the near future, which, however, may not amount to much. It generally betokens the death of some one near, such as a close friend.

HEART

To dream that your heart is paining you, or that you feel a smothering sensation, denotes that some oversight or mental blunder may be the cause of a loss.

HEAVEN

To dream that you are ascending heavenward, denotes that success may come too late in life to bring happiness, consequently a sad ending. To dream that you are climbing to heaven on a ladder and reach the desired spot, denotes that you will rise to great height of power in your present line. To fail in the attempt to climb to heaven, would signify that you are apt to meet with many losses.

HELL

To dream of being in the above place, denotes great temptation that will confront you, which will be hard to resist.

HERMIT

To dream of a hermit, denotes much misery caused by unfaithful friends. To dream that you live the life of a hermit, implies that you are very reserved and selfcentered, and hard to become acquainted with.

HILL

To dream that you are climbing a hill, and reach your objective point, denotes success in a new undertaking. Going down, signifies the reverse.

HISSING

To dream that you hear others hissing you, denotes that you will be greatly displeased at the

doings of a newly made acquaintance. To dream
that you are hissing another, denotes that you are
not truthful to yourself.

HOGS

To dream of looking at the doings of fat hogs,
foretells a change in business which will prove very
good. Lean hogs, foretells trouble with help and
likely difficulties in business. To hear them squeal-
ing, refers to unpleasant news, sometimes death.
To see a litter of them, denotes that there is an
abundance in store for you.

HOMESICK

•To dream of being a sufferer from such, implies
that you will refuse excellent opportunities for
traveling, for which you will afterwards be sorry.

HONEY

To dream of seeing honey, is an omen of much
wealth. To dream of eating honey, denotes happiness in love. To lovers, an early marriage.

HORSE

To dream that you are trying to pass one and
can't, because you are afraid, signifies that you will
forget, or lose a valuable, but will find it again after
much anxiety. To dream that you are riding this
noble animal, is a sign that you will rise a step
higher in the world; but if you are thrown off, it
would refer to scandal and disgrace. To dream of
exchanging horses, denotes that some one will deceive you in a bargain. The selling of a horse foretells a loss; **to buy one**, signifies that **you** will make

money by some speculation, or selling property. To dream that you curry or clean a horse, and that the horse is full of dirt, foretells a coming sickness. To dream of horses in general, is good. The dream of a wounded horse, tells of news of friends who are in trouble.

HORSESHOE

To dream of seeing a horseshoe, is an omen of luck in business; to find a horseshoe, denotes that your interests will advance beyond your wildest expectations.

HOSPITAL

To dream that you are a patient in this institution, is a sign of a disease to break out in your community. To dream that you visit a friend there, denotes that you will hear bad news.

HOTEL

To dream of seeing a fine hotel, denotes riches and much travel. To dream of owning a hotel, denotes a good deal of success, but brought about by your own personal efforts.

HOUSE

To dream that you go through an empty house, signifies trouble. To dream of building a house, you will make a wise change.

HUGGING

To dream that you are hugging one whom you admire, implies that you will have troubles in your love affairs and likely in business. For married people to hug others than their partners, portends toward dishonor.

HUNTING

To dream that you are hunting, denotes that you are struggling for that which you can't gain. To dream that you get that which you are hunting for, denotes that you will overcome your obstacles and conquer.

HURRICANE

To dream that you hear the roar and frightful doings of a hurricane, denotes that you will suffer much torture in trying to avoid business failure. To dream that you look upon the havoc wrought by a hurricane, you will avert some business trouble by sheer good luck, or perhaps through the good advice of some good friends.

HUSBAND

To dream that your husband is in love with another woman, denotes that he will soon tire of his present environments and seek pleasures elsewhere. To dream that your husband is about to leave, and you can't account for it, implies that there is bitterness between you, which has not yet been brought to light. To dream that you are in love with another woman's husband, denotes that you are not happy, and are endeavoring to change your present life.

HYDROPHOBIA

To dream that you are afflicted with such, denotes enemies, who are trying to foil you in your plans. To dream of seeing others afflicted thus, implies that business or conditions will be affected by a death. To dream that an animal in this condition bites you, is a sign that you will be betrayed by a friend in whom you had the utmost confidence.

I

My eyes make pictures when they are shut—
Coleridge.—*A Day Dream.*

ICE

To dream of seeing ice float in clear water, denotes that jealous friends will try to interrupt your happiness, but will not succeed. To dream that you walk on ice, denotes that you will waste much time and money on temporary joys.

ICICLES

To dream of seeing icicles on trees or on buildings, denotes that worry that has been distressing you, will soon vanish.

IDLE

To dream that you are idle; you will fail to accomplish that which you have begun. To see your friends in idleness, denotes a request for assistance from those who are in poverty.

IDOLATRY

To dream of worshipping an image, implies serious mental trouble and ill luck in business.

IMPS

To dream of seeing imps, is a bad omen for those who are ill, or those of advanced years, it refers to serious changes and grave disappointments.

INDIGESTION

To dream of being afflicted with indigestion, forebodes gloomy surroundings, and are given to entertain pessimistic thoughts.

INFANTS

To dream of an infant is an excellent sign, it foretells happiness and joy, good luck and generally successful. Lovers who dream of an infant may be sure of a happy and successful marriage. To a man in business, it foretells a change in business which would be successful. For a woman (unmarried), that she has an infant, denotes that she will be slandered for actions she is not guilty.

INJURY

To dream that you have met with an injury, denotes that your friends will look upon you with favor, and that present wrongs will be righted.

INK

To dream that you are using this fluid, is good, but to spill it, denotes prolonged vexations and many spiteful things to be done through envy. To dream that you have ink on your body, denotes that you will cause suffering and may wrong some one.

INSANE

To dream that you are afflicted thus, forebodes a sad ending to some newly conceived project, also that you may have to contend with ill health. To see others insane, portends that much poverty and misery will prevail among your relations and ultimately seek your assistance.

INTESTINES

To dream of rupturing or suffering in your intestines, denotes family quarrels. To dream of seeing your own intestines, denotes sickness, which will disable you in your daily duties, and thereby suffer an indirect loss.

INTOXICATION

To dream of being in this condition, denotes an increase of wealth and sound body. To dream that you become intoxicated by looking at liquor, is a bad sign, it shows that you are trying to cover your plans by deceptive actions, which may bring you into the police court.

IRON

To dream of being injured by an iron, denotes much confusion in your business. To dream that you touch a red-hot iron, implies that you will have many disappointments in your present doings.

ITCHING

To dream that you itch all over your body, tells of troubles in business, usually caused by enemies that interfere, due to influencing you in the wrong direction.

ISLAND

To dream that you are on an island all by yourself, and if the water be clear about you, signifies pleasant journeys and profitable ventures. To dream of seeing others on an island, denotes a struggle to rid yourself of unpleasant associates.

J

"In Gideon the Lord appeared to Solomon in a dream by night." *1st Kings* iii. 5.

JAIL

To dream of seeing others in jail, denotes that you will be urged to grant a favor, which will be very displeasing to you. For you to dream that your sweetheart is in jail, denotes that you will be disappointed in his or her character, so beware and look well into the matter before you leap.

JAM

To dream that you are eating jam, and if pleasing to the taste, denotes long and pleasant journeys. To dream that you are making it, augurs a happy home and many true friends.

JAWS

To see in your dream the jaws of some large monster, portends toward ill feelings between you and friends. To dream that you are in the jaws of some large beast; many perplexities are lying in your immediate future. To dream that your own is disabled, implies that someone has said a grave falsehood about you.

JEALOUSY

To dream that you are jealous of your sweetheart, or life partner, denotes that enemies are exerting their influence over you to cause you to do wrong. For a woman to dream that she is jealous of her husband, denotes that her actions in home life will give her husband material to make her the butt of ill-timed jests in company.

JELLY

To dream of jelly signifies sorrow and trouble and sometimes that the most hidden secrets shall be revealed and made known.

JEWELRY

To dream of anything in the jewelry line, omens that much pleasure and riches will be yours. To find jewelry in abundance, predicts disappointment.

JIG

To dream of dancing a jig, omens that you are light-hearted and gay, and love your work. To see others dancing a jig, denotes that you are too easy and benevolent, and may give money that will be used for base purposes.

JOLLY

To dream that you are feeling jolly and gay, omens that you will have many friends that look up to you as a leader and entertainer, and thereby have many favors cast your way.

JOURNEY

To dream that you have made a journey and it was a pleasant one, denotes much success and happiness in the near future. If the journey was marred by a mishap; discontent and thwarted hopes.

JUG

To dream of jugs that are full, denotes that you have many true friends, and that they look out for your interest. To dream of taking a drink from a jug, denotes much health and strength, and that you generally look upon the bright side of everything.

JUMPING

To dream of jumping and succeed in getting to where you want to get, omens success; to fail in the attempt, will bring about grave disappointment. To dream that you are jumping over a precipice, denotes bad speculation and troubles in love.

JURY

To dream that you are appointed a juryman, implies that you are highly esteemed by your employees, and may ultimately take one in as a partner.

K

"God came to Laban the Syrian, by night, in a dream, and said unto him, take heed that thou speak not Jacob, either good or bad."—*Gen.* xxxi., 24.

KEG

To dream of a keg, denotes that your present difficulties are principally imaginery, and therefore, it is well not to spoil to-day by yesterday.

KETTLE

To dream of kettles, denotes much difficult work before you. To see kettles that are boiling, omens that your struggle will be soon at end.

KEYS

To dream that you lose your keys; things undreamed of will cross your path. To find keys is a good omen, it speaks of domestic happiness.

KID

To see one at play in your dreams, augurs that you will be careless in your morals or pleasures, thereby breaking some dear one's heart.

KILLING

To dream that you see one trying to kill another, but without success, denotes that you will receive money. To dream that you kill another in self-defense, or kill a beast under similar conditions, denotes victory to the dreamer.

KING

To dream that you see a king, denotes that you are struggling in the wrong direction. For you to dream that you meet a king, denotes a forgiveness for your faults. To have a long conversation with one, implies a conspiracy undermining your efforts from those you trust.

KISS

To dream of kissing the hand of any one, speaks of friendship and good fortune. To see in your dream, children kissing, omens many happy doings. To kiss your sweetheart in the dark, relates to dangers resulting from improper engagements. For you to dream of kissing a strange woman, speaks of loose morals and a deceptive honesty. To dream of kissing illicity, relates to past times that may end dangerously, by giving vent to sexual appetites. To dream that you are being kissed by one whom you are trying to avert, omens a miner illness to the dreamer.

KITE

To dream that your are flying a kite, augurs extravagance, or poor judgment in the dispensation of money matters. Should you fail in making your kite fly, would tell of sad disappointment. To see children fly kites, augurs happiness and success to the dreamer.

KNIFE

To dream of a knife is not good, it refers to quarrels, losses and separation. To dream that you receive a blow from a knife, omens injuries or violence. To dream that you stab another, denotes that you have a poor sense of right and wrong, you should cultivate this faculty.

KNITTING

For a woman to dream that she is knitting is good, it implies that much happiness and peace is hers, and that she will be blessed with many bright children.

L

"And Solomon awoke; and, behold, it was a dream."—
First Kings, iii., 15.

LABORATORY

To dream of being in a place of this kind, denotes danger of sickness, or great energies wasted on fruitless enterprises. To dream that you are experimenting with drugs, and that you are trying some new discovery, and succeed, you will attain great wealth along your chosen line.

LACE

To dream of lace is good; to see your sweetheart wear it, omens sincerity in love and that all will terminate well. To dream that you buy lace, augurs that you will marry a wealthy partner; if married, you will become rich.

LADDER

To dream that you are ascending one, denotes a good fortune, in fact, great success in business. To dream that you fall from one, denotes that your present plans will turn out poorly, the much will arise to discourage you. To descend a ladder; disappointed efforts and desires that are misdirected.

LAKE

To dream that you are alone on a muddy lake, denotes many trials and vexations to be in store for you in the near future. Should the water get into the boat, but succeed in scooping it out, you will eventually overcome your difficulties and come out victorious. To dream of sailing on a clear and calm lake with many congenial friends, denotes much happiness and success.

LAMBS

To dream of seeing a herd of lambs merrily running about, is a happy augury, it denotes an increase in your possessions, and that many good things are awaiting you. To dream of seeing them slaughtered, denotes that you must sacrifice pleasures and infatuations if you wish to reach your desired goal. To dream of having a pet lamb, or that you carry one, denotes much happiness.

LAME

To dream of being lame or seeing one of your acquaintances in that condition, denotes infamy and dishonor for the person afflicted, due to laziness and want of action.

LAMP

To dream of seeing a lamp burning, indicates a rise in fortune and much domestic happiness. To dream that you drop a lamp, your plans and hopes are sure to be shattered. To dream of carrying one, denotes that you are independent and prefer to carry out your own ideas, and seldom take advice.

LANTERN

To dream of seeing a lantern at night in a distance, denotes the receipt of money unexpectedly, if the lantern is suddenly lost to sight, then hopeful plans will take an unfavorable turn.

LAUGHING

To dream that you have been laughing hearty, means success and many happy associates. To hear children laugh, omens joy and health to the dreamer. To hear grown people laugh, a speedy rupture in friendship.

LAWSUITS

To dream of being entangled in a lawsuit, tells of enemies who are trying to influence others against you.

LAZY

To dream of being afflicted with a feeling of inactivity, denotes that some business venture will suffer through lack of attention to details. To dream of seeing others lazy, implies that you will experience much trouble in securing the right kind of help for the conducting of your business.

LEATHER

To dream of seeing piles of leather, denotes good fortune and much happiness.

LEECHES

To dream of leeches, implies that enemies will strive to meddle with your affairs. To dream that they are applied to your body denotes an illness either to yourself or in the family. To see them on others, denotes distress and worry to friends.

LEGS

To dream of the symmetrical extremities of a woman, denotes that you will lose your dignity and act very silly over some insipid creature. To dream that you have a wounded leg, implies a disappointment, possibly a loss. To dream that you have more than two legs, denotes that you have more irons in the fire than you can manage successfully. To dream that you can't use your legs, relates to poverty.

LEMONS

To dream of seeing lemons on trees, denotes that you are upbraiding some one of a charge wrongly, from which you will soon gain proof of your false accusation. To eat them, denotes troubles and shattered hopes.

LENDING

To dream that you are lending money, implies hardships of meeting your obligations, or the payment of private debts. To lend articles, denotes that you may come to want through over-generosity. To refuse to lend, you will gain much of this world's goods and will be highly respected by your friends.

LEOPARD

To dream that a leopard attacks you, implies that while things look flowery at present, you are liable to experience much trouble before you reach the end. To dream that you kill one, denotes conquests in your obstacles. To dream of escaping from one, denotes a present difficulty to turn into joy.

LETTERS

To write them to your friends, or receive them from them, augurs good news, and that you are interested in polite literature, such as poetry, drama, etc.

LIAR

To dream of hearing others call you a liar, denotes humiliations through deceitful friends. For you to call another a liar, implies that you will have cause to regret a former action.

LICE

To dream of the above, tells of much worry and distress. To dream of seeing them on your body, denotes that you will have many vexations and disagreeable obstacles to contend with. To dream of catching them, omens of illness.

LIGHTNING

To dream of seeing flashes and lights in the heavens, preshadows prosperity, but of short duration only. To see the lightning strike some object near you, you will be vexed by backbiters, who will talk ill about you to your friends.

LILY

To dream of lilies, denotes grandeur, power and ambition; to smell them out of season, vain aspirations. To see lilies, growing with their rich foilage, implies to the young, an early marriage.

LINEN

To see it, or handle it in quantities, omens an abundance of riches. To see others dressed in linen garments, denotes joyful tidings, relating to money matters.

LION

To dream of a lion, denotes that you possess strength of character and great determination. To dream that you conquer a lion, denotes a victory over temptation. To dream of a cage of lions, denotes that your success depends much upon your own personal efforts. To dream of being frightened by a lion, tells coming danger, of which you should exercise much care in order to avoid it. To dream that you are defending others from a lion and succeed, foretells that you will baffle your enemies in their plans.

LIP

To dream of thick lips, denotes that the baser world is greatly in evidence in your makeup, and is a warning to fight against low and lusty thoughts. To dream of sweet natural lips, denotes harmony and plenty.

LIQUOR

To dream that you are drinking spirituous liquor denotes that you will have many so-called friends hanging on to you for selfish purposes, also women of a questionable character will seek to win your affections.

LIZARDS

To dream of lizards, denotes unpleasant encounters with enemies. To dream of killing one, signifies that you may regain your laurels. To dream that one crawls up your clothes, you will learn of bad reports from friends whom you sincerely trusted.

LOBSTERS

To dream of lobsters is a happy augury. To see them, forebodes riches and plenty. To dream that you eat them, you will be subjected to an insult, brought about through over familiarity on your part, in some public place.

LOCKET

For a woman to dream that she receives a locket, if unmarried, denotes an early union and that she will be blessed with many happy children. For her to dream that she loses a locket, much sadness will lie in your path.

LOCOMOTIVE

To dream of this iron steed, implies that you are restless and fond of travels, and if the locomotive is in perfect order, your ambition will be crowned. To see one demolished, forebodes distress and many disappointments.

LOOKING GLASS

To dream of a looking-glass, is not a good omen. It generally brings about some undesirable news relating to one's doings. Often friction in the family circle.

LOOM

To dream that you are weaving on a loom, signifies that your life partner will be a thrifty one, and many happy things are to be expected.

LORD'S PRAYER

To dream of saying the Lord's Prayer, implies that your strongest vocation would be in the mental realm, and should concentrate your efforts along the line of some mental work.

LOSSES

To dream that you are losing part of your clothing, denotes that you will entertain a large company, or perhaps, make an address in public, or attract attention in some similar way. To dream of a loss of some valuable, such as a watch or ring, etc., implies that you will regain as much or more than your loss amounted to. To dream of the loss of money would be a similar signification.

LOVE

To dream that your love is not reciprocated, implies that you are bound to feel gloomy over some conflicting proposition, thus causing you to become very undecided, not knowing which way to go, or what to do. If business is the question, listen to your first impulse; be it marriage, act upon your second sober thought. To dream that you love some animal, denotes happiness with what you possess, and are easily satisfied.

LUCKY

To dream of meeting with great luck, is a happy augury to the dreamer. His wishes will be realized and ambition crowned.

LUGGAGE

To dream that you have lost your luggage, forebodes troubles in speculations, and possible family dissension. To the young and unmarried, troubles in love.

M

"In thoughts from the vision of the night, when deep sleep falleth on men, fear came upon me, and trembling, which made all my bones to shake."— *Job* iv, 13-14.

MACARONI

To dream of seeing macaroni in large quantities, denotes that you are inquisitive and will accumulate quite little money. To dream of eating it, as a rule refers to small losses.

MAD DOG

To dream of mad dogs, denotes that you will be greatly annoyed by enemies, who will try their utmost to implicate you in some scandal. If you kill a dog that suffers with rabies you may succeed in overcoming these evil tendencies.

MADNESS

To dream of being afflicted with such a malady, and that you are performing extravagant actions in public, implies that there is sickness ahead of you; you should avoid carelessness relating to catching cold. To see others afflicted on like manner, denotes fickleness in friends.

MAGICIAN

To dream of seeing a slight-of-hand performer, augurs that the dreamer will travel much and possess keen observation, and is extremely fond of the super-natural.

MAGPIE

To dream of this sister bird to the crow, speaks of quarrels that will leave very unpleasant tastes behind. Further, it is well for the dreamer to exercise care in his manner and conduct after such a vision.

MAN

To dream of a man with a fine physique, tells of great satisfaction and joy brought about through rich possessions. To dream of a man with a sour expression and ill-formed, implies that you will meet with many disappointments and perplexities.

MANUSCRIPT

To dream that you are at work on a manuscript and succeed in finishing it, denotes that your ambition will be reached; but to dream of an unfinished manuscript, denotes disappointments. To dream that you have a manuscript returned, forebodes unpleasant criticisms regarding your actions.

MAP

To dream of studying a map, or looking up some location, implies that you nay soon contemplate a change. To dream that you can't locate the place you are looking for denotes a disappointment.

MARBLES

To dream that you are playing marbles, denotes that scenes will be enacted in and about your place that will take you back to your childhood's happy days.

MARINER

To dream that you follow a vocation of this nature, denotes many travels to the dreamer, many to foreign lands, and much pleasure will accompany these trips.

MARRIAGE

To dream of contracting a marriage, denotes happy times. To be married; unexpected perils. To see a marriage; sickness, melancholy. To marry an ugly person; death, or some serious disaster. A handsome person; joy, happiness and great advantages. To marry your own wife; much profit. To wed a virgin; honor without profit. To espouse one's sister; serious entanglements. To marry a servant; others are endeavoring to deceive you.

MARTYR

To dream of suffering martyrdom in a good cause, forebodes honors and public probation.

MASON

To dream of a mason at his duties, augurs a rise in your present circumstances and that those you associate with will be more agreeable than heretofore. To dream of seeing a body of men belonging to the order of masons, rigged out in full uniform, speaks that too many are depending upon you.

MATCHES

To dream of seeing matches, denotes that some one will bring you happiness and contentment. To strike a match, unexpected good news relating to your business.

MATTRESS

To dream of such, refers to new duties that are near at hand, that you will be requested to perform. To dream of sleeping on one, denotes that your environments will cause you to entertain much that is to your liking.

MEADOW

To dream that you are in a meadow, portends that you will accumulate much valuable property, and that your married life will be one of joy.

MEALS

To dream that you see a meal placed on a table, denotes that you will let the little things in life interfere with the big things, and thereby wasting much good time.

MEASELS

To dream of being afflicted with this malady, signifies much anxious care and tribulations. To see others suffering with them, augurs that you will be requested to aid some charitable affair.

MEATS

To dream of meat that is raw, implies that much trouble and discouragement is ahead of you. To dream of cooked meat, denotes that you have a rival for the same thing you wish to gain. To see it putrid and maggoty, is a sign of sickness and death.

MEDICINE

To dream that you are taking medicine with difficulty, forebodes troubles and distress. If it tastes good, an ailment that you will soon outgrow.

MELON

To dream of melons, denotes that your truest friend that you have, you are laughing at, and making him think less of you. To dream of eating them, denotes that you judge too quickly; disposition is what will make or mar your life.

MENAGERIE

To dream of visiting such a place, denotes trouble. If you are single and jealous, denotes that you will be miserable during your married life.

MENDING

To dream of mending an old garment, denotes that you will never attempt to abuse any trust again, and the wrongs that you have done heretofore, you will endeavor to right, as you are a person of honor. To dream of fixing clean garments, you will make some gains in the way of a speculative nature.

MERRY

To dream of feeling merry, to the unmarried denotes that a distinguished foreigner is hoping to meet you with a view to matrimony. To the married, much success and gains near at hand.

MICE

To dream of mice speaks of family troubles and friends who are insincere, and business may take a change for the worse. To let them escape, implies, that you will foil your enemies. To feel a mouse in your clothing, your would-be friends are seeking to scandalize you.

MIDWIFE

To dream of a midwife, forebodes that an illness is threatening you, which will almost bring you to death's door. Much care should be exercised regarding your physical condition after a dream of this nature.

MILK

To dream that you are drinking milk, is a very good dream, it speaks of peace and plenty and many pleasant travels. To dream of spilling milk, relates to slight unhappiness in the home, usually brought about by continually finding fault with one another.

MILKING

To dream that you are milking, and experience much difficulty in relieving the milk from the cow's udder, denotes that possessions are withheld from you, which you will win by holding your own and not be persuaded to compromise. If the milk flows without the least effort on your part, implies to good fortune.

MINE

To dream that you are in a mine, and meet no difficulties in going about it, denotes prosperity. To dream that you are lost in one; danger of failure in business. To dream of owning one, denotes that trouble will arise where pleasure was anticipated. To dream that you are working a mine, implies that an enemy is endeavoring to meddle with your possibilities.

MINISTER

To dream of a minister, foretells that your friends are true and hold you in high esteem. To hear one preach, implies that you will assume new duties that will be highly criticized by others.

MINUET

To dream of dancing the minuet, augurs success and many joys. To see it danced, denotes companions who are congenial and very sincere in their actions toward you.

MIRROR

To dream that you are looking into a mirror, forebodes many discouraging issues. To see others looking into a mirror, denotes that others will worm themselves into your confidence for their own selfish motives. To dream that you break one, augurs bad news bearing the death of a loved one.

MISER

To dream that you see a miser counting his hoard, usually relates to the gains of money. To dream that you are miserly, speaks of unhappiness from those who are highly inflated with their own importance.

MOLASSES

To see molasses in your dream, relates to pleasant doings, and many happy surprises. To dream of eating it, denotes unhappiness in your closest affections, brought about by the actions of a rival.

MONEY

To dream that you receive money, denotes good business, prosperity. To dream that some one tells you that you will receive money, foretells disappointment in money that you expect. To dream of finding it, signifies worries, ultimate good to come therefrom. To pay out money; possible losses. To lose it; unhappiness in family affairs. To count it, and find a deficit; troubles in meeting payments. To steal money; you must guard your actions. To save money, augurs comfort and plenty. To make false money; shame and blame. To dream of swallowing money; reverses may make you avaricious.

MONKEY

To dream of a monkey, implies that deceptive associates will flatter to advance their own interests. For a young woman to dream of this animal, denotes that her lover may deem her unfaithful, consequently it would be advisable for her to insist on an early marriage. To dream of caressing a monkey, signifies that your confidence will be betrayed by one whom you thought true.

MOON

To dream of seeing the moon in brilliant clearness; to a wife, love and much happiness; for a husband, a sudden rise in money matters. To see the new moon, an advantageous change in business.

MORGUE

To dream that you are going through a morgue looking for some one you know, implies bad news, likely the death of a relative. To find many corpses there much bitterness will be poured in your cup.

MORTGAGE

To dream of giving a mortgage, augurs financial troubles ahead of you, which will cause you many **unhappy nights in trying to think your way out.** To dream of holding a mortgage against another, denotes that you have covered the worst period in life relating to money matters.

MOSQUITO

To dream of killing mosquitoes, denotes that you will frustrate the plans laid by your enemies. To see them, or be annoyed by them, you will suffer a loss at the hands of enemies.

MOTHER

To hear your mother cry, omens illness either to you or her. To dream of leaving her, relates to troubles, in which you will have great difficulties in releasing yourself. To dream of her after a long absence, denotes a making up of an estrangement between you and relatives. To see her dead; troubles to you or to your business. To see her dead in reality and you dream of speaking to her, denotes happy tidings. To hear her call you, implies that you are not following the right business. To see her with face drawn and haggard; disappointment.

MOUNTAIN

To dream that you go along a high mountain, and come across a sharp precipice and are compelled to turn back, prognosticates troubles and vexations. To dream that you ascend a mountain successfully implies that you will rise to wealth and prominence. If you fail to reach the top, you may look for reverses; you must be more firm and determined and the future will be brighter.

MOURNING

To dream that you are dressed in mourning, or see others dressed so, is a sign of an early wedding in your family, or near relation, to which you will be requested to help to arrange and conduct the affair.

MUD

To dream that you see others covered with mud, signifies that you will meet some one that will bore you very much. To walk in mud, omens that you will lose confidence in one whom you trusted in the past. To dream of having mud on your clothes; others are talking ill of you.

MULE

To dream of a mule, denotes that you will be vexed by the mental stupidity of others. To ride one; great anxiety in your daily pursuits. To be kicked by a mule, speaks of upheaval in love and marriage.

MURDER

To dream of seeing a murder committed, augurs that you will have to face many misdeeds caused by others, also that you may learn of the violent death of one whom you know. To dream that you are committing this deed, implies that you are following work that will ultimately cause the loss of your reputation. To dream that you are being murdered, omens that others are undermining your interests.

MUSIC

To dream of sweet music, augurs prosperity and much happiness. Music that is displeasing to the ear denotes friction in the household affairs, that requires tact in order to adjust it.

MYSTERY

To dream that you are inveigled in some mysterious affair, denotes that you will be hounded and goaded into an affair by strangers that will produce many complications.

N

"And he dreamed yet another dream, told it to his brethren, and said, 'Behold, I have dreamed a dream more; and, behold, the sun and the moon and the leven stars made obeisance to me.' "—*Gen.* xxxii, 9.

NAILS (Finger Nails)

To dream that you have long nails, augurs great profit. To dream that they are cut very short; trouble, dishonor, losses and family difficulties. To see them torn off; much misery, affliction losses and unhappiness in the family circle.

NAILS (Of Iron)

To dream of rusty nails forebodes illness, and slowness of business. To see a lot of nails, prognosticates many laborious duties to perform.

NAKEDNESS

To dream that you suddenly discover your nudity and are trying your utmost to conceal it, denotes humiliations as the result of indulgence in illicit pleasures. It is a warning to curb or control those desires. To see yourself nude, refers to unwise associates that may prove disastrous. To dream (for a man) that you are running and suddenly lose your clothes, denotes trouble from a woman whom you dislike, by forcing her presence on you, or by blackening you in the eyes of her own sex. To dream of seeing others nude, denotes that designing persons are trying their utmost to induce you to leave the straight and narrow path.

NAVEL

To dream of your navel being painful or swollen, refers to unpleasant news as to father or mother, danger of death according to the amount of pain experienced. If the dreamer has neither father nor mother, it relates to suffering and sorrows from deprivation of an inheritance.

NAVY

To dream of anything relating to the navy, usually refers to long journeys, victorious undertakings, and joyful recreations. To dream of a dilapidated navy, prognosticates many struggles and untruthful friends.

NECKLACE

To dream of losing a necklace, augurs sorrows, due from early bereavement. For a woman to dream that she receives a necklace, implies to many happy things from her husband; many joyful hours in the home.

NEED

To dream that you are in need, indicates that you must be careful or you may make some unwise venture that will have a distressing ending. To dream of seeing others in need, denotes that you will suffer unexpectedly through over-benevolence.

NEEDLE

To dream of using a needle, is generally an indication of bickerings, which will be the cause of your suffering keenly through unsympathetic feelings. To find a needle, augurs to useless anxieties. To dream of threading a needle, forebodes that you will be greatly annoyed by the trials and ill luck of others.

NEIGHBORS

To dream of seeing your neighbor, shows much time will be wasted in idle gossip. Should the neighbor appear sad and vexed, would denote dissension that would be lasting and bitter, and neither one would care to humble themselves to make up.

NEPHEW

To dream of seeing your nephew prognosticates dangerous rivals in both affection and business. To experience difficulties with a nephew, implies that you will have great obstacles in adjusting disagreeable surroundings.

NEST

To dream of finding one or to see one that is empty, denotes poor ending of business. To dream of finding a hen's nest, relates to domestic affairs, such as contentment, also that you will be blessed with many happy and healthy children. To dream of a nest containing bad eggs, omens a disappointment.

NETTLES

To dream of treading on nettles or being stung by them, denotes that you are restless and never satisfied with your position; always complaining of your fate. You must be more firm and determined and things will look brighter.

NEWSPAPER

To dream that you are reading a newspaper, augurs deceit, falsehood, and that fraud will be detected in your dealings, thus jeopardizing your reputation to a certain extent.

NIGHT

To dream that you are walking at night, denotes that unexpected hardships may attend you in your immediate undertakings, but should you see the night vanish before you, your hardships will turn to good account.

NIGHTMARE

To dream that you experience such a feeling, means that disputes and worriments will confront you. For the unmarried, it would mean that disappointment would be their lot.

NOISE

To hear a peculiar noise in your dream, prognosticates news that is not very pleasing to you. Should the noise succeed in arousing you from your slumber; a change for the better can be looked for.

NOSE

To dream of seeing your own, signifies that you have more friends than you think; you are admired for your character and sympathetic nature, your love of nature is exceedingly strong.

NUMBERS

To dream of numbers and are unable to recollect them, denotes that business will cause you uneasiness on account of its unsettled condition. To recollect them implies good fortune in store for you.

NUNS

For a woman to dream of a nun, augurs widowhood or perhaps a separation from her lover. For a man to dream of such, denotes that his materialism is over-powering his spirituality.

NURSE

To dream of nursing a child, denotes an illness to some member of the family. To dream that you are a nurse, implies that you will occupy a position of responsibility and trust.

NYMPH

To dream of nymphs bathing in clear water, denotes many gay pleasures to be realized, and the good viands of your friends festal board will tickle your palate with delight. To see them out of water, would denote a disappointment.

O

"Then thou scarest me with dreams, and terrifiest me through vision."—*Job*. vii, 14.

OAK

To dream of seeing a tall well-leaved oak, omens riches and happiness and that you will live to a green ripe old age. To see an oak tree full of acorns, speaks of a rise in your condition. For the lover to dream of oaks, refers to an early marriage.

OATH

To dream of taking an oath, is an invariable sign of complications and vexations in your immediate future.

OATMEAL

For you to dream of oatmeal, forebodes many happy conditions, to eat it, much health to enjoy your good fortune.

OBITUARY

To dream of reading a friend's obituary, implies that news of a very unpleasant nature will soon reach you. To dream of writing one, many uninteresting duties will be thrust upon you to perform.

OCEAN

To see the ocean calm in your dream, is good, for the business man it denotes splendid remuneration, and the young will bill and coo harder than ever. To dream of being on a stormy sea, refers to troubles in business and friction in the household. To sail on calm waters is good. To watch a rough sea from shore, implies that enemies are talking disrespectful of you.

OCULIST

To dream of having cause to consult an eye-doctor, forebodes that your present occupation is displeasing to you and a change would be advisable.

OCULTIST

To dream of an ocultist, denotes that you will be compelled to repair some fault, or an injury to acknowledge. To dream that you are studying or going to become an ocultist, augurs that pleasant returns will reach you for the kindness you have shown to others.

OFFENSE

To dream that your actions have given offense to the sensitive feelings of others, predicts many obstacles in your way before your ambition is crowned. To dream that others offend you, signifies that others are criticising your actions unjustly, which will cause your temper to rise and appear on the surface.

OFFERING

To dream of making some liberal offer for the benefit of christianity, signifies a desire to return or lead a better life. To give meagerly, denotes that after you have tried to return to virtue, temptation will overtake you and fall back into the old channel.

OFFICER

To dream that an officer enters your place and you feel confident that he has legal papers to serve, and does so, denotes unpleasant and discouraging news from those whom you expected to hear different.

OFFSPRING

To dream of your own, signifies happiness, and that your parental love is strong. To dream of seeing the young of animals, predicts energies that will bring about prosperity.

OIL

To dream of oil spilled about, denotes irreparable losses. To see it on yourself; profit and gain. In large quantities; your excess in pleasure may cause you to suffer.

OLIVES

To dream of olives, is propitious, if you eat them, augurs many true friends. To gather them; many favorable results in business.

OMNIBUS

To dream of riding through the streets in such a vehicle, implies to ill-doings of friends, which may ultimately cause an estrangement.

ONIONS

To dream of seeing many onions, relates that your success in life will bring about much envy and spite. To eat them is good, it augurs victory over obstacles.

OPERA

To dream of seeing one, predicts many good friends, and through their influence you will attain much that is good in life. To appear in one; hatred and jealousy, due to your dignified and independent ways.

OPIUM

To dream of this fateful drug, predicts that others are endeavoring to injure you in your prospective plans, through underhand methods.

OPULENCE

To dream of fairy-like opulence, signifies that the dreamy lacks strength of character: no determination. He should cultivate application, continuity and power of decision. To dream of solid wealth without any "froth," is propitious and will live to realize the real thing.

ORANGES

To dream of seeing oranges on trees, is an excellent omen, it augurs an abundance and a happy condition. To eat them, generally refers to illness, or tidings of one who is convalescent. To dream of buying them implies that complications will wax into profit.

ORATOR

To dream of becoming enthused with an orator's eloquence, denotes that an appeal will be made to you for aid, and the appealer's tremulous grief in his tone of voice will reach your heart completely. For a woman to dream of being in love with an orator, denotes that she is indolent, impressionable, sentimental and overfond of luxuries.

ORCHARD

To dream of passing through an orchard that is bearing fruit, predicts happiness and prosperity. To pass through a barren orchard; much trouble to gain your coveted object in life. To dream of gathering fruit, success is sure to smile on you.

ORCHESTRA

To dream of hearing an orchestra play, augurs that things will greatly pick up in the near future, and remain very encouraging thereafter. To dream of playing in one; your sweetheart or wife will radiate much sunshine.

ORGAN

To dream of playing an organ, predicts much happiness and worldly comfort, also that your position in life is mapped out for you. To hear an organ played with selections that appeal to the heart; lasting and devoted friendship. To hear doleful strains, you will soon learn of happenings that will weary you.

ORNAMENTS

To dream of receiving an ornament, denotes a contemplated change that should be carried out. To give one; guard your extravagance. To lose an ornament; a loss, a friend, or something material.

OSTRICH

To dream of this bird, denotes that you will amass possessions through your effusive kindliness and diplomacy, mingled with deceptiveness that will ultimately be up against you. To catch one; many travels and interviews with people of note.

OVEN

For a woman to see her oven overheated, denotes many dear friends far away which ultimately may cause her to leave her home and move where they are. For her to dream that she is baking, augurs slight disappointments.

OWL

To dream of hearing the weird and solemn sound of an owl, is a sign that a bereavement will soon shatter the nerves of the dreamer. To see this nocturnal creature, implies that enemies are watching with designs.

OX

To dream of seeing a fat ox, predicts good times and felicity near at hand. Lean ox; poor times and little reward for your efforts. To see them fight; an indication of an early quarrel.

OYSTERS

To dream of seeing them served on the table, denotes friendship. To eat them raw, is a splendid sign of excellent health and fine success.

P

In bliss, in dream, in silent night.
There came to me with magic might,
With magic might my own sweet love,
Into my little room above.—HEINE. *Youthful Sorrows.*

PAGE

To see a page in your dreams, denotes that your marriage will turn out a mesalliance. You should make sure whether the prospective partner is worthy of you before taking the step. To dream that you are a page, implies that you will commit some petty affair that will bring you remorse.

PAIL

To see a lot of empty pails in your dream, predicts an unprosperous condition. To dream that you see a pail, or carry a pail, and it is filled with something, denotes that success will be with you, and much that is pleasant to look upon.

PAIN

To dream that you suffer pain, forebodes unhappiness, and that you will regret some trivial affair not worth bothering about. To see others suffering thus, denotes that you are cherishing a mistaken ambition.

PAINT

To dream that you are covered with paint, denotes that your pride will be injured through unjust criticism of others. To dream of admiring beautiful paintings, augurs that friends whom you thought sincere hold you up in the wrong light. To dream that you are painting yourself, implies energy and vitality wasted on an object that will bring you little or no reward. For a woman to paint a picture, predicts that the person she admires adores someone else.

PALACE

To dream that you are in a palace and are delighted with its grandeur, denotes that you will meet with much public favor. To see one only from the outside, would foretell, uneasiness, vexations and jealous rivals.

PALL-BEARER

To dream that you act in this capacity, forebodes humiliation by the constant attacks of enemies. To see a pall-bearer, denotes you will make yourself disliked by expressing your convictions.

PALMISTRY

For a young woman to dream of palmistry denotes that she has strong psyhic force and has the power to divine good things for others. For a man to dream of this ancient and much abused science, foretells that with his optimism and philosophy he has the power to encourage the disheartened on to success. To dream of having your plams read, predicts that you have many friends at heart, but openly may condemn you. Should you dream of reading palms, or that you have read the palm of another, augurs riches and fame for you. To dream of reading a clergyman's hand, denotes that your forte is in the mental realm, and can sway a crowd better than an individual.

PANCAKE

To dream of making pancakes, forebodes that your commonsense and thrifty qualities will lead you on to good fortune. To eat them, implies that some new venture will end very propitiously.

PANTOMINE

To dream that you are performing such, denotes slight unpleasantries that will be a stumbling block for a short period. To see others perform thus, some indiscrete friend will blab on you.

PARALYSIS

This is a dream that is bad in whatever form it may be brought about. It denotes money troubles, misery, long illnesses, and bitter disappointments to the dreamer. To lovers, affection that turns cold and dies away.

PARASOL

For a married person to dream of this sunshade, predicts infelicity that will ultimately bring about disaster. For the unmarried to dream thus, means a desire to flirt and fond of admiration.

PARCEL

To dream of receiving a parcel, implies a surprise from one whom you least expect. To lose one; a proposition will fail to come to a head.

PARDON

To dream that you are incarcerated for an offense of which you are innocent and seek pardon, forebodes present troubles that will ultimately prove to your advantage. To dream that your punishment is just; obstacles will be yours.

PARENTS

Should your parents be dead in reality, and appear to you in a dream, forebodes troubles, you must exercise care in the planning of affairs. To dream of living parents, and see that they are happy and well, denotes fortunate changes to the dreamer.

PARK

To dream of going through a beautiful park, predicts pleasant happenings to the dreamer. To a lover, the park will glide smoothly on the matrimonial sea.

PARROT

To dream of a parrot, means a discovery of a secret. For the unmarried to dream of owning a parrot; lovers quarrels may be looked for.

PARTING

To dream of parting from friends that is affecting, implies that little things will annoy you much.

PARTRIDGE

To dream of this bird, forebodes intimacy with ungrateful females. To kill them, means that you have the power of acquiring but not accumulating wealth. To eat them, and if they seem to tickle the plate; enjoyment and success.

PASTE

To dream of paste on your clothes, denotes that others whom you are dealing with hide their bad traits in order to win your confidence and gain their selfish end through your instrumentality. To dream that you are pasting, predicts, that matters you thought were adjusted have to be gone over again.

PASTRY

To dream of making pastry, augurs pleasures and profit. To see it, denotes that some cunning person is seeking to deceive you. To eat it, forebodes many happy gatherings among friends.

PATENT

To dream that you have conceived a patent, denotes to the dreamer that he is a man who seeks, reasons and calculates and wants positive proof before going ahead. To dream that you tried to conceive a patent and have failed, predicts that you reason things to death, you should listen more to your first impressions.

PAUPER

To dream that you are in this deplorable condition, refers to a sudden and unexpected rise. To dream of seeing others in this condition, denotes that you will be requested to offer aid.

PAVEMENT

To dream that you are walking on a pavement and it goes down carrying you with it, but escape unhurt, denotes a new business prospect soon to open which is good and should be carried out.

PAWN SHOP

To dream that you have pawned articles, denotes that family jars are staring you in the face, in which you are to blame. To redeem an article that has been pawned, would indicate many efforts that were directed in the wrong direction, but are now on the right track.

PEACHES

To dream of eating peaches in season; much satisfaction and enjoyment. To dream of them out of season, would mean many trials and disappointments.

PEACOCK

To dream of seeing one spreading his tail; wealth and an indication of a very handsome partner. For a woman to dream that she owns a peacock, denotes that she is placing too much confidence in a certain person; be careful of how much of your past you unlock. To dream of pulling his beautiful feathers, denotes that you will fail to accomplish a certain object due to your proud spirit.

PEARLS

To dream of pearls is propitious, it augurs excellent business and not much to annoy you. For a girl to dream of receiving a string of pearls from her lover, means many good things for her. For her to dream of breaking her pearls would imply deep sadness through misunderstanding. To lose them would mean about the same.

PEARS

To dream of eating pears in season, forebodes happiness and joy, particularly so if they be nice and ripe. To dream of green or decayed pears, sickness and disappointment.

PEAS

To dream of eating them, and if they are luscious to the taste, denotes a rise in business with quick returns. To dream of eating them raw would imply, vexations and disappointments.

PELICAN

To see a pelican in your dream, relates to success but of slow order. To dream of catching one, you will thwart an enemy before he has much ground to work.

PENALTIES

To dream that you are compelled to pay a penalty, refers to loss and sickness. To dream that you get off free, augurs honors and distinction. To dream that they are going to impose a penalty on you, denotes that you will be mixed up in a fuss, due to some argument.

PENITENTIARY

To dream of being a convict in such a place, denotes that you will have many petty things to annoy you. To escape from one, you will conquer those that are against you. To dream of a penitentiary, forebodes that you will have duties to perform that will be most disagreeable.

PEOPLE

To dream of a crowd of people at a fashionable affair, denotes many pleasant things to the dreamer. To dream of a boisterous crowd of people, predicts that conditions will prove very discouraging to you, perhaps brought about through family jars. To dream of seeing many people in a well-behaved condition, is always good; to see them otherwise, augurs trouble of some kind.

PEPPER

To dream of pepper is not good, it relates to worry, fretfulness, irritation, and the coming in contact with one who is hard to get along with.

PERFUME

To dream of perfuming yourself, denotes that you will hear of many complimentary things said about you. To dream of receiving perfume as a present, predicts many gains and that you will associate with people of intelligence. To smell it, is as good.

PERSPIRATION

To dream that you are perspiring freely, denotes that the burdens that have been weighing heavily upon you will soon appear, and will prove to those who have been gossiping ill of you, that you are not as bad as they painted you.

PETTICOAT

For a young woman to dream that she is losing her petticoat in some public place, denotes that her lover is growing indifferent towards her. The dreamer should be more reserved and self-centered and keep the other side guessing, for a man loves to pursue and wants that which is hard to get. To dream of a petticoat with many inharmonious colors; many petty annoyances are to be confronted. To dream of a very rich and expensive petticoat, denotes pride and dignity.

PHANTOM

To dream that such an apparition pursues you, but you succeed in getting away, denotes joy and freedom from present worriments. To touch you; unpleasant experiences to the dreamer. To see one in black; troubles from a woman. To see one running away from you; troubles are at an end.

PHEASANT

To dream of this bird, denotes much happiness. To kill one, denotes that you must fight against a certain temptation. To eat one, denotes that your high living and overeating will produce functional trouble, such as a weak digestive apparatus.

PHOTOGRAPH

To dream that you are having your pictures taken, denotes that you will be taken for some one else and experience much embarrassment. To see pictures, denotes happiness. To see yourself in a fancy pose, implies that backbiters are talking ill of you. To dream that you are taking photographs, predicts that your love for the beautiful is interfering with business.

PHYSICIAN

For a girl to dream of a doctor, implies that she is entertaining frivolous thoughts that may lead her into temptation. To dream that she is sick, and has the doctor, denotes that sorrow will soon cross her path. For a married woman to dream of a physician, denotes that she lacks self-control and gives vent to her imaginary ailments.

PIANO

To dream of hearing piano music, if it be pleasing, denotes joy and contentment. Discordant music; possible family disputes. For an unmarried woman to dream that she is playing difficult music, predicts a conquest in love with an indifferent lover.

PICKLES

To dream of pickles, means efforts misdirected and energy wasted, or that you do not follow your work because your heart is in it, merely from a sense of principle or duty. To dream of pickles also tells of troubles in love, but not necessarily separation. For a girl to dream of eating pickles, denotes many rivals for the object of her heart.

PICKPOCKET

To see a pickpocket in your dream, forebodes that an enemy will annoy you much and cause others to hold you up in the wrong light. To dream of having your own pockets picked, denotes that a friend will become an enemy through the spiteful actions of others.

PICNIC

To dream that you help to make merry at a picnic, implies to rises and ultimate success. To dream that your merry-making at a picnic has been interrupted through some cause, means that your plans will not mature quite as favorably as anticipated.

PICTURES

To dream that you are making pictures, denotes much labor with small profit. To see them; surprises but unexpected friends.

PIES

For an unmarried woman to dream of baking pie, signifies that her love for admiration and desire to flirt may lead into temptation. To dream of eating them; enemies are talking disrespectful of you.

PIG

To dream of fat and healthy pigs, denotes that your energies will be rewarded. To dream of lean and sickly looking pigs, means much hard work and efforts that will prove fruitless.

PILLOW

For a woman to dream that she is making a pillow, denotes peace and plenty and that she will abound in luxuries. To dream of many beautiful pillows, predicts a love for romance and sentiment.

PIMPLES

To dream of having them on your body, augurs much wealth, both in real estate and personal. To see them on others is an indication of disgust, due to the woes that are being retailed by others.

PINS

To dream that another is trying to prick you with a pin, but succeed in warding off the attempt, denotes a surprise. For instance, something that you have asked for, you will get a great deal more than you expected. To dream of swallowing a pin, denotes that unforeseen circumstances will lead you into unpleasant conditions.

PIPE

To dream that you crawl through a long dark and rusty sewer pipe after one you love and experience a smothered feeling, denotes a bitter disappointment. To dream of smoking a pipe, augurs that you will meet an old acquaintance whom you thought was cross with you. To see a lot of old broken pipes (iron), poor business.

PISTOL

To dream of shooting off a pistol, denotes that you will accuse another on mere hearsay for which you will be sorry and subjected to an apology. To dream of these firearms in general, forebodes struggles.

PITCHER

To dream of a pitcher, denotes a loss, generally due to your own carelessness, sometimes that of others. To dream of a broken pitcher, refers to the loss of friends.

PLAGUE

To dream of a place where a plague is raging, implies to poor business, terminating in thorough discouragement. Even the home may be shattered due to poor business. To dream that you are afflicted with it, denotes that you will become confused mentally over conditions. This is a warning that you must not lose self-control.

PLANE

To dream that you are planing, denotes that your efforts will be rewarded and your ambition crowned. To see others working with a plane, forebodes good conditions relating to business in the near future.

PLANK

To dream of walking across a plank safely, denotes that a pending project will turn out propitiously. To dream of crossing a rotten plank and it breaks down with you, augurs distress and unhappiness.

PLAY

To dream of attending a play, relates to short-lived pleasures. For the unmarried to dream such, denotes that their sweethearts will act indifferent and cause you to think that there are others whom they like better.

PLOW

To dream of seeing persons plowing, denotes good fortune and that you are on the high road to success. To dream that you are plowing yourself, predicts splendid rewards for your efforts.

POCKETBOOK

To dream that you find a pocketbook filled with money is an excellent omen for your immediate success. To find one that is empty, denotes shattered hopes.

POISON

To dream of seeing others poisoned, denotes an illness generally brought about through a contagious disease. To dream that you are poisoned forebodes news from the absent that is painful and distressing to you. To dream that you are preparing to poison someone, denotes many plans that you thought fruitful will turn to naught.

POLICE

To dream that a police is seeking to arrest you for a charge you know nothing of, denotes that you will win a race relating to business condition. To feel that you are guilty of a charge, denotes the conclusion of bad business.

POLISHING

To dream that you are polishing up articles that are rusty and bad looking, and succeed in so doing, implies that you will rise to great height of power in a business way. If your efforts are without results, struggles and disappointment.

POOR-HOUSE

To dream of a poor-house, denotes friends who may apparently conduct themselves very truthful, but in reality are only seeking you to further their own selfish purpose.

PORCUPINES

To dream of seeing a porcupine, forebodes disagreements relating to business undertakings. For the unmarried to dream of a porcupine, predicts a delicate affair relating to a sweetheart.

PORTRAIT

To dream of admiring a beautiful portrait of some one you know, denotes long life to that individual. To give, or receive one, predicts deceptive flattery from our near associates.

POTATOES

To dream of potatoes in general, augurs good. To dream that you are planting potatoes, denotes that your ambitions will be crowned. To dig them; excellent omen for success. To eat them; your gains will be large and many.

POULTRY

To dream of live poultry, denotes much valuable time wasted on frivolous pleasures. To dream of dressed poultry, predicts that your generous ways will bring you many friends that will stick by you while the money last.

PRAIRIE

To see a prairie in our dream, denotes luxuries and clear sailing and that you are much sought after by others. To dream that you are lost in one, portends to sadness and disappointments.

PRAYER

To dream of saying your prayers, denotes dispute and difficulty among friends. To dream of seeing others saying their prayers, predicts joyful happenings.

PREACHER

To dream that you are a preacher, or are preaching, signifies that plans will fail to materialize. To dream of hearing a preacher preach, signifies discontent brought about through the fault finding of others.

PRECIPICE

To dream of falling over a precipice, denotes great outrage and peril for the dreamer. To dream of being on the edge of a yawning precipice, relates to losses and calamities.

PREGNANCY

For a husband to dream of the pregnancy of his wife, and in reality such is the case, denotes a safe delivery, and little suffering to the wife. For a woman to dream that she is pregnant, implies that friction and misunderstanding will be the chief obstacle in life. For a virgin, or unmarried woman to dream of being pregnant, is a warning that she contemplates a marriage that may prove disastrous.

PRIEST

To dream that you are confessing to a priest, implies to humiliation caused from unjust publicity. For a young woman to dream that she is in love with a priest, implies that she is placing confidence in one who does not mean what he says.

PRISON

To dream of a prison usually denotes misunderstandings with friends that will cause you much uneasiness. To dream of being in prison, denotes troubles and disappointment to the dreamer.

PROMENADE

To dream that you are promenading, denotes that you will engage in business that will highly reward you in your efforts. To see others promenading, means keen competition in business.

PROPERTY

To dream of receiving property as a gift, implies to prosperity and ultimate gains. To dream of losing property, foretells that your affairs will suffer at the hand of those who failed to carry out your instructions.

PROSTITUTE

To dream of being in company of a prostitute, denotes that others will condemn you for things of which you are guilty. To dream of being hounded by one denotes that you are a favorite among the opposite sex and that they hold you up as an idol.

PRUNES

To see them on trees, or eat them, denotes joy. Dried prunes would relate to vexations. To dream of them out of season; obstacles and trials, but only of a short duration.

PUDDINGS

To see pudding made, denotes good returns from a source you expected very little. To dream of eating pudding, troubles and disappointments.

PULPIT

To dream that you speak from a pulpit, or that you are in a pulpit, denotes sorrows and discontentment due to poor business.

PULSE

To dream that you feel the pulse of another, denotes that your actions will be discovered and laid to public criticism. To feel your own pulse, is a sign that your nervous system needs an overhauling.

PUMP

To dream that you are pumping water and the water is clear, you will have much to be thankful for, as joy and success are yours. To dream of seeing others pumping, forebodes that influence is much sought after by those who are less successful than you.

PUNISHMENT

To dream of undergoing punishment of some nature, denotes success and wealth but not of a lasting character. To cause another to be punished, portends that you are given to malicious mischief.

PUP

To dream of pups, forebodes that you will derive much joy from your friends as you will have many that are true. This is especially true if the pups are healthy and cute. Should they be lean and sickly looking, the reverse of the above would be the case.

PURCHASE

To dream of making a purchase, denotes that you will forget, or misplace something that you will need badly, however, not necessarily a loss.

PURSE

To dream of finding a purse containing money and some other valuables, forebodes that you will receive money that you are really looking for.

PYRAMID

To dream of climbing a pyramid, denotes that you will take a lengthy journey ere long, one that will afford you much pleasure and joy. To dream of seeing one, implies to wealth and joy and a possible rise in the near future.

Q

"And it shall come to pass afterward, that I will pour out my spirit upon all flesh; and your sons and your daughters shall prophesy, your old men shall dream dreams, you young men shall see visions."—*Joel* ii., 28.

QUAIL

To dream of quails is considered a very favorable omen. To dream of killing them, would portend begrudging tendencies shown by your friends. To dream of eating them, implies to your over generosity, which should be held in check.

QUARANTINE

To dream that you are held on this account, forebodes many mean deeds by malicious evil-doers.

QUARREL

To dream of quarreling with a stranger, denotes that you will shortly make a new acquaintance with one whom you wish you had not met. To quarrel with a friend, implies that you will soon have an agreeable time with that friend. For lovers to dream of quarreling, predicts that they will bill and coo harder than ever.

QUARRY

To dream of falling into a quarry, forebodes that you will suffer much at the hands of enemies. To dream of working in a quarry, denotes that your success is only gained after much hard labor and careful saving.

QUARTETTE

To dream that you belong to, or are singing in a quartette, denotes that harmony and congenial surroundings will make life worth living.

QUEEN

To dream of a queen, is propitious. It speaks of success in recent ventures. To dream of one who has lost her beauty, denotes disappointments.

QUESTIONS

To dream of asking a question, denotes that your integrity is much sought after and will be the means of rising to a high and trusted position. For you to question another implies that deceptive friends are working you harm.

QUICKSAND

To dream of sinking in quicksand, denotes trouble and worriments caused by the deceit of others. To see others in quicksand, denotes that you will frustrate the plans of one who tried to work you harm.

QUININE

To dream of taking quinine, means renewed energy that will spur you on to meet your troubles. To dream of giving it to others; returns from hopeful prospects will be meager and uncertain.

QUOITS

To dream of playing quoits, foretells an ambition that is slow in realization. To see others play, denotes that your success will depend much upon your power of concentration.

R

"And being warned of God in a dream that they should not return to Herod, they departed into their own country another way."—*Matthew* ii., 12.

RABBITS

To dream of rabbits is good. Conditions are sure to move along smoothly and bring good returns. To the lover, it denotes a proposal through a letter; accept it; happiness is yours. For a married woman to dream of these animals, foretells an increase in the family.

RACE

To dream that you are running a race and win, fortells conquests in business affairs: to lose in one, implies that your efforts are being interfered with by others.

RADISH

To dream of radishes, denotes that your ambition will be swiftly realized. To dream of eating them, forebodes that you are destined to suffer through the betrayal of others.

RAGE

To dream that you are in a terrible rage, denotes that you will have quarrels with friends, which may terminate in bodily harm. To see others carrying on in this manner, denotes that business affaire are sliding along in a discouraging rut. For an unmarried woman to dream of being in a rage, implies that that she is mistaken if she thinks her lover is true.

RAILROAD

To dream of a railroad generally refers to travels. If the road is clear; safe journeys. To see an obstruction, forebodes unpleasant journeys, and in business unfavorable turns. To dream of walking on a railroad, denotes worries and disappointments.

RAIN

To dream of being in a soft rain without any storm, portends good things to the dreamer. To dream of being in a terrible rainstorm, forebodes losses and vexations to the affluent and good things to the poor.

RAINBOW

To see a rainbow in your dream, omens good things to the dreamer. Lull in business will turn to a more promising aspect. For sweethearts to dream of the rainbow denotes that their union will bring happiness and contentment.

RAISINS

To dream of eating raisins, denotes a realization of wealth and joy. Wealth however may come slow but sure.

RAM

To dream of being bucked by one of these animals, denotes that you will be reprimanded by one whom you failed to perform duties as per request.

RAPE

To dream that this act is perpetrated on one whom you know, denotes that scandal will assail your ears relating to dear friends. For an unmarried woman to dream that she has been the victim of such, implies that she will hear damaging news, relating to her lover.

RASPBERRIES

To dream of raspberries, in season augurs good. To a man of business success due to his own determination and strict attention to business. For an unmarried woman to dream of raspberries, omens that her lover will be industrious and a good provider.

RATS

To dream of rats is a bad sign of loss by theft. To hear them gnawing is unusually bad. For a girl who has a lover to dream of rats, it is a warning for her to be cautious with her person in order to protect her honor.

RAVEN

To dream of ravens, relates to unhappy conditions in business affairs. To kill them, denotes a quarrel due to your defiance and resistance.

RAZOR

To dream of sharpening a razor for the sole purpose of fighting with another, augurs conflicts that may prove disastrous. To dream of cutting yourself, you will have enemies to content with.

REAPERS

To dream of seeing reapers in the field and busy performing their task, and the object is fruitful, implies prosperity and great joy. To dream of seeing them idle, denotes in a present undertaking efforts practically without results.

REFRIGERATOR

To dream of a refrigerator, denotes that you will injure a friend's feelings in your entertaining, by acting selfish. You will be spoken of discourteously, regarding your conduct.

REINDEER

To dream of this animal, denotes many true and devoted friends. To drive one denotes a gain in business, through the prestige of outside people.

RELICS

To dream of relics is a warning to be careful of some household valuable. To dream of receiving a relic, denotes that you will break or spoil something that you priced highly.

REPTILES

To dream of reptiles that appear harmless and that you like to watch their graceful movements, denotes a settlement of money that you had thought was as good as lost. To dream of seeing them vicious and wanting to attack you, implies to enemies that will renew their bitterness towards you. To dream of killing reptiles, forebodes that you will overcome great obstacles. To handle them without harm, omens that the bitterness of friends will be restored into pleasure and happiness.

RESIGN

To dream that you have resigned your position, predicts that a change is in store for you shortly, which will be advantageous.

REVENGE

To dream of revenging yourself, denotes a heartless nature on your part. This tendency will be the cause of losing many a good friend through your conduct.

REVOLVER

To handle a revolver in your dream is not good, it relates to quarrels and strife. You should cultivate more self-control. For an unmarried woman to dream of this fire arm, denotes an interference in her closest affections.

RHUBARB

To dream of this vegetable, denotes that you are of a jovial nature and many seek your company and listen to your philosophy. To dream of eating it means that present plans will culminate propitiously.

RIBBON

To see a display of ribbon in your dreams, denotes a happy and jovial nature and can throw cares aside at will. For an unmarried woman to dream of ribbons, denotes that her sweetheart is only sowing his wild oats, so do not be too exacting; he will be alright by and by.

RICE

To dream of eating rice, signifies domestic bliss and business success. To see a quantity of rice, implies to prosperity in all trades and many warm friends.

RICHES

To dream that you are rich, denotes that your aggressive and firm nature will bring you much that you justly deserve.

RINGS

To dream of seeing rings on your fingers, implies to new ventures, which generally turn out good. To see rings sticking in the ground with only the settings visible and pick them out, denotes disappointments, relating to business. For an unmarried woman to receive a ring, augurs that an old love affair will be revived and end in a union.

RIOT

To see a riot in progress, augurs disappointments. To dream of seeing some one killed that you know, predicts poor conditions in business.

RIVAL

To dream of having differences with a rival, denotes that you are weak and wavering in decision and afraid to assert your right. To succeed in ousting your rival, denotes you to be a splendid leader and should follow a position of leadership.

RIVER

To dream of a clear and tranquil river, is a lucky omen, particularly for people in a professional calling. To dream of a river that is undulating, forebodes jealousy and discontentment. To see a river overflow its banks, if the water be clear, denotes the meeting with a person of distinction. To see muddy water in a similar condition, foretells that indifferences have to be adjusted caused through the indiscreet actions of others.

ROAD

To dream of following a straight and easy road, denotes joy and prosperity. To find yourself on one that is winding and hard to follow up, denotes changes that will not prove very propitious as much annoyance will attend them.

ROCKS

To find yourself climbing on rocks and succeed in reaching the top, denotes joy and happiness. To dream that you fail to reach the top, denotes reverses and obstacles.

ROOF

To dream of being on a roof, augurs success. To find much difficulty in getting down, denotes that your success is of an uncertain nature. To dream of seeing others on a roof and are unable to get down, implies to petty vexations.

ROOSTERS

To dream of a rooster is a happy omen, it relates to great success, but the success may have a tendency to make you vain and unbearable in your action, and thus the loss of the good wishes of others.

ROPES

To dream of climbing a rope, and succeed in reaching the desired spot, augurs that you will overcome enemies. To fail in climbing the rope successfully, foretells interferences from one whose friendship was not elected but forced on you. To dream of walking a rope, denotes that you will succeed in some speculation. To see others walking a rope, augurs gains through the kind assistance of friends. To dream of jumping a rope, predicts that you are looked up to by your friends as congenial, and are well liked.

ROSES

To dream of seeing beautiful roses in season, denotes that success is heading your way, it also speaks of pleasurable events. For an unmarried woman to dream of gathering roses, denotes an early proposal from her ideal.

ROWING

To dream that you are rowing in a boat with others, denotes that you will derive much pleasure from gay and worldly associates. Should the boat you are rowing capsize, forebodes that you may face monetary difficulties, due to a lull in business. To win in a race; honors will be yours. To lose; your rivals in love will outshine you.

RUINS

To dream of a ruin, implies to unexpected gains. To dream of being among ruins; discoveries leading to success. To dream of ancient ruins, refers to extensive travels in foreign lands..

RUNNING

To dream of running fast is an excellent omen. Your plans will materialize and much will be brought your way. To stumble or fall; disappointment. After an enemy; victory, great profit if you apprehend the enemy. To run naked; trust violated by relatives. For a sick person to dream of running, omens disaster to the dreamer. For a woman to dream of running nude; dishonor and loss of friends.

S

"And the King said unto them, I have dreamed a dream, and my spirit was troubled to know the dream."—*Dan*. ii., 3.

SAFE

To dream of a safe, denotes that you are exempt from the struggles that usually go with business. To dream of opening, or working the combination of a safe, denotes a disappointment, relating to business matters that you had counted on as good.

SAILING

To dream that you are out sailing on calm waters, augurs excellent success in whatever attempted. To be on ruffled and murky water, predicts unpleasant happenings that will thwart your energies.

SAILOR

To dream of seafarers, predicts unpleasant and exciting journeys by water. For an unmarried woman to dream of a sailor as her suitor, denotes struggles through her over anxious desire for admiration.

SALAD

To eat salad in your dream, denotes that you will be highly bored by disagreeable people. For an unmarried woman to dream of making it, denotes that she should insist upon an early marriage as her lover is changeable and fickle.

SALMON

To dream of salmon, often refers to troubles in the family. To eat it, predicts altercations with neighbors.

SALT

To dream of salt, forebodes troubles and strife with close associates. To dream of spilling it, enemies will accuse you openly of wrong doing. To an unmarried woman the dreaming of salt means many lover's quarrels through jealousy on her part, due to the sweetheart talking about women she dislikes. Heed not what he says thereby giving no chance for an argument.

SASH

For young and unmarried woman to dream of wearing a long sash, denotes that her sweetheart is true but conceals his affections for obvious reason.

SATAN

To see some form of a satan in your dreams, relates to business plans that may prove futile. To dream that you are fleeing from Satanic Majesty, denotes that you will conquer your enemies and convert them into the best of friends. To dream of being punished by satan, is a warning against soft palavars who are endeavoring to warm themselves into your confidence.

SAUSAGE

To dream of making them, is a warning of excess regarding sexual appetite. To eat them, augurs love intrigues. To see them in large quantities; carnal desires.

SAW

To dream of working with a saw, predicts industry and energy that will bring about an abundance. To dream of seeing others working with a saw, forebodes gains that were thought irreparable.

SCAFFOLD

To dream of a scaffold, denotes disappointments that will greatly wound your dignity. To examine one, implies to deceit from those whom you always trusted.

SCALES

To dream that you are weighing yourself on a scale, denotes an increase in your conditions, and that pending investments will bring flattering returns. To see others weighing themselves, portends that you lack decision and depend too much on what others have to say.

SCHOOL

To dream that you are young and attending school, indicates distinction in some mental line. To dream of visiting a schoolhouse, where you once attended, implies to petty annoyances relating to present business.

SCISSORS

To dream of scissors, augurs trouble. For the married it tells of jealousy and suspicion. To sweethearts quarrels and accusations; a love that won't run smooth.

SCRATCH

To dream that you have a bleeding scratch on you, denotes that enemies are endeavoring to destroy our property, if the scratch does not bleed they will be foiled in their plans.

SCREECH-OWL

To dream of hearing the peculiar notes of this owl, implies to some bereavement, usually the death of a near relative.

SCULPTOR

To dream of one who follows this art, augurs a change in your vocation, generally to one of great importance and one that will command more respect.

SCYTHE

To dream of this ancient implement, denotes that some unforseen circumstances will prevent you from following your duties properly. To dream of one that is old and worn out, means troubles with friends, due to bluntness on your part.

SEA

To dream of hearing the moaning of the angry sea, foretells a lonely life due to your reserved and selfcentered tendencies. To dream of the sea, denotes pleasant and happy travels. For an unmarried woman to dream that she is calmly on the sea with her lover, denotes connubial bliss.

SEAL

To dream of seals, denotes a very extravagant taste that will be the cause of much hardship late in life. It is a warning that your extravagance is abnormal and that you should moderate it.

SEDUCER

For an unmarried woman to dream of being seduced, denotes that she is too sentimental and impressionable. The dreamer should cultivate more strength of character and fixed purpose in life. Should a man dream of betraying a girl in this manner, implies that accusations will be hurled at him falsely, from which he may suffer great humiliations.

SERENADE

To dream of hearing a serenade, denotes that you will receive pleasant and delightful news from those who are away. To help to serenade; splendid things are in store for you.

SERPENTS

To dream of serpents, generally denotes enemies and ingratitude from friends. To see them curl, twist and crawl, denotes hatred and illness. To kill them; victories over enemies. To capture one, you'll succeed in destroying that "green-eyed monster" jealousy.

SERVANT

To dream of discharging a servant, implies to losses and proceedings that you regret. To dream of quarreling with one, denotes that you are too intimate with your help, show more dignity and make them look up to you.

SEWING

To dream of sewing and fixing things over, denotes disappointment in pleasure relating to less. To dream of sewing something brand new joy and contentment are yours.

SHAMPOO

To dream of seeing some one being shampooed, denotes that you are requested to perform a duty that is below your dignity. To dream of having it done yourself, denotes that you must be more secretive, or you will arouse suspicion regarding your doings.

SHAVING

To dream of being shaved and the shave is close and easy, denotes that a near friend will favor you by paying a debt that you owe in order to help you out of difficulty. To dream of shaving yourself, predicts that you will contract a debt innocently or perhaps overdraw your bank account.

SHEEP (See Lamb)

To dream of seeing a flock of sheep, denotes much good to the dreamer. To see them lean and scraggy looking, denotes involvement brought about through poor financing. To dream of cutting their wool; rewarded efforts.

SHELTER

To dream of seeking shelter against rain, relates to secret troubles. To seek shelter from storm, denotes that your hopes in your present plans will drift into despair.

SHERIFF

To dream that you succeed in eluding a sheriff, denotes that you are carrying on plans that are not legitimate, however, will prosper for a certain time. To dream of being apprehended by a sheriff, implies that present uneasiness will terminate into joy.

SHIP

To dream of a ship in perfect condition, is good. To dream of a ship in great distress in angry waters, denotes troubles in the conducting of your affairs, or that some intrigue will come to light from which you will never regain your good name. To see others shipwrecked, augurs anxieties for the wrong doing of another. To dream of being shipwrecked yourself, denotes peril or loss of good name.

SHIRT

To dream of taking off your shirt, predicts an estrangement with a loved one. Generally due to your inconsiderate actions. To see your shirt torn in your dream, relates to pleasant surprises. To lose it; troubles in business or affairs of the heart. To dream of a shirt that is soiled, predicts a nervous system which needs a hauling over.

SHOES

To dream of shoes that are badly worn or ill kept, denotes that you lack tact and are too blunt and outspoken, consequently you make enemies. To dream of having them shined, omens prosperity and happy incidents. To see your shoes untied, augurs disagreements in friendship. New shoes;

good news, hope to be realized. For a young woman to dream that a gentleman removed her shoes, denotes that the dreamer must be cautious, for her lover may make advances, or ask for liberties.

SHOOTING

To dream that you are shooting, denotes misunderstandings between friends. To hear shooting; ruffles in the domestic circle and to sweethearts, quarrels of a temporary nature.

SHROUD

To dream of a shroud, predicts unhappiness and a tendency to illness, from which business may suffer. To dream of seeing the removal of a shroud from a dead person, omens strife and contention from a source you least expect.

SICKNESS

To dream that you are sick, denotes sadness and the coddling of sorrow. To attend the sick; joy, profit and happiness. To see a member of your family sick; an unexpected pleasure that will terminate in sadness.

SILK

To dream of silk in any form is a happy augury, your ambition will be crowned, and happiness reinstalled where strife existed. The dreamer of silk is usually possessed of much pride.

SILKWORM

To dream of a silkworm, implies that you are contemplating a new venture, which will prove very successful. To see them shedding their cocoons, denotes success after many obstacles experienced.

SILVER

To dream of silverware, implies that the dreamer is too materialistic and takes little interest in the spiritual. Material pleasures seem to hold sway. To dream of silver money, implies vexations relating to the meeting of obligations.

SING

To dream that you are singing, denotes that your happy moments will be converted into sorrow. To the unmarried, suspicion and jealousy may step in and destroy their happy dreams. To hear others sing, omens happy tidings and pleasant moments spent with cheerful companions.

SKATING

To dream of seeing skating, denotes humiliation from the hands of those who are envious of your position by not properly guarding their tongues. To dream that you are skating, denotes that you are about to make a change which you will have cause to regret. Think twice before you act.

SKELETON

To dream of seeing a skelton approaching you, forebodes sad and shocking news. To dream of seeing a skeleton remaining motionless, implies enemies undermining your efforts.

SKULL

To dream of skulls, is a sign of family squalls and a general reminding of one another's short comings.

To the unmarried; quarrels due to fickle and changeable natures. To dream of a skull of one whom you know, augurs injured pride.

SLEEP

To dream of seeing others sleeping, denotes that you will succeed in accomplishing your object. To sleep with a person of repulsive ugliness, implies to sickness and displeasure. For a young woman to dream of sleeping with a handsome man; troubles, annoyances and possible loss. To sleep with a woman, if married; troubles to your wife, or family, if single, danger of treason, or that you will yield to the wiles of a designing woman. To dream of being discovered with another; denotes disappointment relating to money matters.

SLIDING

To dream of sliding down a deep sideling, denotes that you are too gullable and may suffer a loss by placing too much confidence in an affair of business. To slide in general, implies disappointments. To the lover; differences over trivial affairs.

SMOKE

To dream of being in, or suffering with smoke, denotes injury through the machinations of false friends. To see smoke, false glory.

SNAIL

To see a snail crawl in your dream, relates to an honorable charge. To see one with long horns, infidelity, adultery and fond of ribald talk. To step on one, you will meet people that you wish you had not.

SNAKES

To dream of snakes, as a rule implies to evil in some form or other. To dream that a snake bites you, signifies a quarrel with a friend or relative. If a snake winds about you and you are unable to conquer it, tells of an enemy that will deeply provoke you. To dream of being surrounded with these reptiles and succeed in only killing one out of many, signifies that some one will cheat, or "do" you in money matters. To succeed in killing every snake about you, omens that you will have a great power over your enemies. To walk over them without trying to kill them, denotes that you are wearing out your nerves by useless anxiety and false apprehension. To dream that they bite you; you will yield to evil actions through enemies. To dream of handling them and they seem playful and harmless, implies that you are inventing a plan with which to deceive those that oppose you. To step on snakes without biting, denotes that you will be bored by those you thought were interesting.

SNOW

To dream that you are in a snow storm, denotes disappointment, regarding a pleasure which you have looked forward to with great enthusiasm. To dream of seeing dirty snow, predicts that your pride will be lessened and you will recognize those whom you once thought were beneath you. To dream of being snowbound; many obstacles and hard pulls before success is reached. To see the ground with a few inches of beautiful snow denotes joy and pleasure. To eat or taste it, good health.

SOLDIER

To dream that you are a soldier, augurs that your ambition will be crowned. To see a wounded soldier, denotes that the distressing conditions of others will cause you sympathy to fight against your better judgment. To see them marching; promotion. For an unmarried woman to dream of a soldier, is a warning to resist immoral advancements.

SON

For a father to dream of his son as being fine looking and healthy, or anything that is propitious about him, denotes that he will make his mark in the world and gain much honor for his sterling qualities. For a mother to dream of her son about anything that is good, the above can be used as an intrepertation. To dream of him in distress, refers to grief, loss and sorrow.

SOUP

To dream of eating soup, foretells comfort and happiness. To see others eating it; few obstacles in your attempts.

SOWING

To dream of seeing others sowing, portends to advancement. To sow yourself, hopes to be realized.

SPARROW

To dream of these little aggressive and bold friends, denotes that neighbors are coveting your possessions or begrudge your success.

SPIDER

To see spiders in your dreams, denotes that thrifty and conscientious tendencies will be the power of amassing a large fortune. To dream of killing one, signifies quarrels and hatred. For a young woman to dream of having a pet spider, predicts that she will marry a professional man.

SPLINTER

To dream of running a splinter in your body, denotes petty annoyances from friends.

SPOONS

To dream of a spoon, portends happiness and much domestic bliss. To dream that you are filching a spoon, denotes that your company manners do not correspond with your home manners.

SQUIRREL

To see squirrels in your dream, denotes a pleasant surprise, also rising conditions in business. To dream of having one for a pet; happiness and contentment. To kill one, lack of tact.

STAGS

To dream of stags implies that you have many true friends and your power behind the curtain is in much demand in gatherings and organizations.

STALLION

To see a fine stallion in your dream, implies that you will rise to honor and riches. To dream of riding one and he is gentle you'll gain much distinction in a localway.

STARS

To dream of seeing them clear and brilliant; good news, prosperity and pleasant journeys. Shooting or falling stars; sorrow.

STARVING

To dream of seeing others in a starved condition, implies to vexations and hard to make headway in a financial way. To dream that you suffer in this manner; unexpected good fortune.

STATUARY

To dream of these sculptured figures and see them in abundance, denotes a present from one whom you thought had lost all esteem for you.

STEALING

To dream of catching a woman who is in the act of stealing and hold her until an officer arrives, but through her smiling and congenial expression of goodness the officer refuses to punish her and sets her free, portends that you will reveal a secret of your past life that some day you will greatly regret. To dream that you have stolen something and afterwards are discovered with the goods, but give up your booty to the owner and all is forgiven, denotes that you will receive money unexpected. To accuse others of stealing, denotes that you lack consideration in your actions towards others.

STEEPLE

To dream of seeing a high steeple on a church, implies to an uncertain physical condition, a warning to the dreamer of an illness. To dream of climbing one, and success in reaching the top; success and honor. To fail on reaching the top; difficulties of a large variety.

STILLBORN

To dream of a birth of this nature, relates to discouraging incidents and many things to distract our attention from your regular routine of work.

STILTS

To see others walking on stilts, augurs uncertainties in business conditions. To be on stilts yourself; an opposition from others relating to a venture.

STING

To feel a sting of an insect in your dream, implies to unhappiness due to over exacting habits from others.

STOCKINGS

For a woman to dream of beautiful stockings, denotes that she is fond of admiration and encourages men's attention through her actions. To see your stockings torn, denotes that she will barter her body and soul, or at least will be tempted in this direction for financial reward, a warning, to resist temptation.

STORE

To dream of a large store filled with goods, augurs success through rapid advancement. To dream of being in a large store; pleasure and good fortune. To dream of working in one; your success is brought about through your own personal efforts and hard work.

STORM

To dream of hearing the whistling of a storm, and if the storm leaves ruin in its wake; business troubles and frictions with friends. Should the storm pass by without any damage, the above indication will be greatly ameliorated.

STRAWBERRIES

To dream of this fruit is good, it tells of success in love and a happy marriage. To eat them; joy, honor and security in business.

STREET

To dream of wandering in a street aimlessly, denotes mental anxiety, and that you may become discouraged in your life work. To dream that you are walking the street in a happy mood; your desired goal will be realized. To dream of being on a dark street and experience feeling of fear, but are not molested, denotes success after strenuous efforts.

STRUGGLING

To dream that you are engaged in a struggle; difficulties to combat with. To dream of coming out victorious; success due to your firm determination.

SUFFOCATING

To dream that you are suffering thus, implies to sorrow due to the coldness and indifference of one whom you deeply love. To see others in this manner; you are being imposed upon your kind nature.

SUGAR

To dream of eating sugar, denotes that you will experience things that are not as sweet as your dream, but your perseverance will aid you in plowing to your goal.

SUICIDE

To dream of rushing out of the body, denotes that your reserved and self-centered tendencies cause people to misjudge you. To see another commit suicide, augurs that losses and reverses of others may directly effect you.

SUN

To dream of seeing a bright sun, denotes the discovery of secrets for the betterment of business. To see it rising; good news. To see it setting; false news pertaining to losses. To dream of the sun is conceded good for those who have strife, or to do with enemies.

SURGICAL INSTRUMENTS

To see such instruments in your dream, denotes much worry and outlay of money for illness and accidents that may occur in the family.

SWAN

To dream of large and beautiful white swans, on clear and quiet waters; prosperity and pleasant happenings. To dream of black swans; pleasure that will bring disgrace and loss of name.

SWEARING

To dream of hearing others swearing, portends to obstacles in business. To lovers; interferences in their closest affections.

SWEETHEART

To dream that your sweetheart is amiable and good natured, portends that the bark will glide smoothly on the sea of matrimony. To dream of a sweetheart that is displeasing and unprepossessing; happiness will vanish and estrangement appear.

SWIMMING

To dream that you are swimming and possess great ficility in the act, besides the water being clear, speaks of much success in your business. To dream of swimming under water, or that you go up and down; struggles and mortifications.

SWORD

To dream of wearing a sword is good, it relates to distinction. To dream that a friend hands you a broken sword, portends troubles by the hands of the law, where your defense will be ignored and dealt with little or no compassion. To dream of seeing many swords; indifferences to be adjusted.

T

"And it came to pass at the end of the two full years, that Pharoh dreamed; and behold, he stood by the river."—Gen. xii., I.

TABLE

To dream of a table loaded with appetizing viands, denotes the indulgence of gay pleasures. To dream of clearing a table, implies to pleasures that will wind up in difficulties. To dream of eating from a table, augurs happiness and comfortable circumstances. To dream of breaking one; disappointment.

TAIL

To dream of seeing the tail of an animal, implies to vexations over trivial affairs. To dream that you possess a long tail similar to that of a beast, foretells a gloomy outlook, relating to a new project. To dream of cutting a tail, denotes that you must guard your tongue when in society.

TAILOR

To dream of a tailor measuring your body for a suit of clothes, implies to pleasant surprises. To dream of a tailor at his work, denotes perplexities connected with your duties. To have troubles with a tailor; slight losses.

TALISMAN

To dream of receiving a charm of this nature, augurs gains due to the honest advice of a friend. For an unmarried woman to dream of receiving a charm, portends that he will be the one of her lover's choice.

TALKING

To dream of some one who acts as if he wanted to talk to you, but fails to do so, denotes that a seemingly prosperous scheme will come to naught. To dream that you are talking to others, denotes early worries will disturb your mind. To hear people talk, or feel that they are talking about you, predicts that you will be accused of aiding the downfall of another.

TAMBOURINE

To dream of seeing others using this instrument, or to hear its sounds, denotes pleasant surprises mingled with a gradual rise in business. To dream of dancing to one; great delight.

TAPESTRY

To dream of seeing beautiful tapestries, denotes culture and refinement, and that you are extravagant in your taste. To dream of possessing them; riches will be yours. For an unmarried woman to dream of them; a brilliant marriage.

TAPEWORM

To dream of suffering with a tapeworm, denotes you to be nervous, restless and excitable and let imagined illness carry you away. To see one; disappointment.

TAR

To dream of having tar on your hands, or clothes denotes disappointments and vexations. To see it in large quantities; troubles caused by enemies.

TATTOO

To dream of seeing another tattooed, denotes that the success of others will hurt your feelings and depreciate your abilities. To see yourself tattooed, implies to family estrangements.

TAXES

To dream of being unable to meet your taxes, or feel that they are too high, denotes that you will be pressed unduly in the meeting of an obligation. To pay them and feel satisfied, denotes hopes to be realized.

TEA

To dream of tea in general, denotes financial difficulties that are a drain on your resources and a burden to your mind. To drink it; pleasures that will burden you. To see others drink it; your aid will be solicited in helping an unfortunate.

TEARS

To dream that you are overcome by emotion and shed tears, augurs sorrow. To see others in tears; your suffering will arouse the sympathy of others.

TEASING

To dream of teasing another, augurs that your cleverness is much sought after by your friends. To dream of being teased; joy and contentment, and prospective popularity.

TEETH

To dream of having false teeth and take them out of your mouth, implies to dental work that will either be painful or not satisfactory. To dream that your teeth are worn down to the gums, denotes quarrels that will terminate in disgrace with a close associate. To dream that your teeth are loose; unpleasant things to content with. To lose them; trials will rob you of your pride. To have them examined, a warning to be on the alert for enemies. To dream of having poor teeth; money troubles. To spit them out; illness and sorrow in the family. To dream of one tooth being longer than the rest; affliction on account of a parent. To have one fall out; sad news. To dream that your teeth are white and beautiful and in reality are not; joy, health and prosperity. To dream that your teeth are so long that they annoy you; quarrels and possible law-suits.

TELEGRAM

To dream of sending a telegram, predicts that you will have difficulties with an intimate friend, who in turn will talk ill of your business. To dream of receiving one, is an indication of receiving profitable news.

TELEPHONE

To dream of talking over a telephone, denotes rivals, both in business and in love.

TEMPEST

To dream of tempest, implies to controversies with friends, misfortune is also predicted. To dream of being thrown down by tempest, denotes malicious planning among enemies.

TEMPTATION

To dream of resting with temptation, augurs troubles of some kind. If you succeed in resisting temptation, denotes success after much hard work.

TENT

To dream of seeing a city of tents, signifies changes in territory. To dream of being in a tent augurs a change in business. If the tent is strong and secure, the change is for the good.

TERROR

To dream of being terrorized of some object, denotes disappointment. To see others suffering thus; sad news from friends to their sorrowful predicament.

THAW

To dream of seeing ice disappear in this manner, relates to pleasure and profit. To dream that it is thawing from under you, denotes energies directed in the wrong direction.

THEATER

To dream of being in a theater relates to pleasant and congenial friends. To dream that you are an actor in a theater, denotes an early change, which will prove profitable. To dream of being in one during a fire, signifies a change that will not be profitable.

THIEF

To dream of thieves entering your house and robbing you, denotes profit and honor. To dream of catching one of these intruders and succeed in bringing him to justice, augurs shrewdness on your part in deceiving your enemies. To dream that you are a thief and followed by officers, denotes business troubles.

THIGHS

To dream of admiring your thighs, augurs pleasure and good cheer. For a young woman to admire them, predicts that her frivolity and selfishness may lead her to take a false step.

THIRST

To feel thirsty in your dream, denotes that you are very aspiring and love to lead. To dream of quenching your thirst; your love for leadership will be rewarded.

THORNS

To dream of seeing thorns, denotes that your neighbors are envious towards you. To dream that thorns are on your body; you will be tormented. To dream of being pricked with them, troubles with the dreamer's employment.

THREAD

To dream of unraveling thread, denotes the discovery of a secret. To dream that you tangle it; you will confide a secret to a friend who is indiscreet, consequently it will become public property.

THRESHING

To dream that you assist in threshing grain, and the yield is plentiful, denotes prosperous business and much joy. To see others threshing; you will enjoy great pleasure from the benevolence and wealth of others.

THROAT

To dream of cutting another's throat, denotes that you will harm a person unconsciously. To dream that your throat is cut; hopes and success will be shattered. To dream of a well developed throat; success. To have a sore throat; anxiety.

THUNDER

To hear thunder in your dream threatens troubles in business. To see the elements in wild commotion and the vivid lightnings flash; loss of wealth, or wounds.

TIGER

To dream of a tiger, denotes jealous and furious enemies. To succeed in warding it off; efforts to be crowned. To kill one; complete triumph.

TIPSY

To dream that you are in this "happy" state, denotes that you are very optimistic and take life as it comes. To dream of seeing others in this condition, denotes that you are too thoughtless of the future.

TOADS

To dream of these hopping creatures, omens misfortune of some kind. To kill one, implies that you are too rash and fool hardy. To play with one, you will be misjudged by a friend.

TOBACCO

To dream of tobacco is a happy omen. To dream of smoking tobacco; much pleasure. To chew it; good news, To see it grow; success in business.

TOMATOES

To dream of tomatoes is good. To dream of eating them; splendid health. To gather them; happiness in marriage. For the unmarried to dream of tomatoes, augurs a smooth sailing on the sea of matrimony.

TOMB

To see a tomb in your dreams, denotes regrets. To help build one; birth of children. To fall into one; sickness and misery in the family. To read the inscription on one you'll have to perform duties that are unpleasant.

TONGUE

To dream that you see your tongue, or that your tongue is very large, means that you are misunderstood and accused wrongly for your actions. To dream of seeing the tongue of another, gossip will assail your ear that is detrimental to your character.

TORTURE

To dream that you assist in torturing others, denotes that plans you thought propitious will prove fruitless. To dream of defending others from torture; success after much hard work. To dream that you are tortured yourself, implies sorrow due to the doings of deceptive friends.

TRAGEDY

To dream of a tragedy, denotes of friends and wealth. To dream that you had to do with a tragedy, implies to personal miseries and profound regret.

TRAIN

To dream that you are riding on a train, implies to good news relating to some contemplated project. To dream of making a train and just miss it, denotes that present complicated affairs will ultimately prove a source of benefit to you. To dream of being on top of a train, and reach your destination successfully; gains, prosperity. To drop off, or fail to reach the desired place, disappointments and vexations.

TRAP

To dream of catching game in a trap, denotes success. To dream of being caught in a trap; enemies will succeed in their plans. To set a trap yourself, implies that your plans or deceptive actions will be discovered.

TRAVELING

To dream of traveling on foot; much hard work before you. By carriage; profit and pleasure combined. By train; hopes to be realized. By water; prosperous and happy. To dream of traveling pleasantly and smoothly is propitious.

TREES

To dream that you are climbing a tree and reach the top with ease is propitious. To fail, and obstacle to contend with. To fall from a tree; misery and sickness. To see them green; hopes to be realized. To cut one down; lack of sense relating to spending of money.

TRICKS

To dream of seeing tricks performed, denotes gaities, and happy surprises. If with cards and you can see through or detect the trick, business matters will adjust themselves.

TRIPLETS

To see triplets in your dream, foretells that your judgment is good and is a warning for you to go ahead with your plans.

TROPHY

To dream of trophys that you have won, or that were presented to you, implies to an advancement gained through amiable and courteous demeanor.

TROUSERS

To dream that you got trousers on wrong side out, denotes the forming of an attachment of which you will find it difficult to resist. To dream of trousers refers to guilty intrigues that may never come to light.

TRUMPET

To hear the blowing of a trumpet, denotes startling news that is near at hand. To blow it yourself, ambition to be crowned.

TRUNK

Trunks as a rule relate to journeys. To dream of packing your trunk; you are soon to make a trip. To dream that your trunk is too small; you are to be promoted shortly. To see your clothes scattered all about the trunk instead of being in the trunk, you will change to a place where you will be dissatisfied and will return, sorry that you changed.

TUNNEL

To dream of going through a tunnel while on a train, omens an illness and a possible change in business. To dream of being in a tunnel and meeting a train, foretells unhappy conditions, relating to business. To dream of being in a tunnel and there meet with difficulties is always a bad dream.

TURNIPS

To dream of a large patch of turnips, augurs that things will soon begin to look better. To dream of eating them, portends toward illness to the dreamer. To prepare them; success due to your selfmade abilities.

TURPENTINE

To dream of seeing turpentine, augurs unhappiness in the near future. To dream of using it on one for medical purposes, denotes great favor won from those whom you befriended.

TWINS

To dream of healthy twins, augurs business success and many happy hours at your fireside. Sickly twins; sorrow and discontent.

U

"And Joseph dreamed a dream, and he told it his brethren; and they hated him yet the more." —Gen. xxxvii., 5.

UGLY

To dream of being ugly, signifies misunderstandings between loved ones. In business, things are inclined to drag. For a woman to dream of being unattractive, signifies that her cold and indifferent action will cause her friends to think less of her.

UMBRELLA

To dream of umbrellas, augurs that petty trials will ultimately come to a head and annoy you very much. To dream of lending one; destroyed confidence. To borrow one, you will distrust a friend which will ultimately bring about an estrangement. To dream of having the storm turning it wrong side out, denotes vexations from others who endeavor to belittle your reputation.

UNCLE

To dream of an uncle of yours, relates to news that is displeasing to you. To dream of seeing your uncle afflicted or in a bad predicament, denotes family quarrels.

UNDRESS

To dream of seeing others undress, denotes that your joy and sweet satisfaction will end in an uncertainty. To see yourself undress, you will learn bad reports about you. For a woman to dream of undressing in the presence of others, denotes that false reports regarding her conduct will greatly annoy her.

UNIFORM

To dream of wearing a uniform, denotes distinction in your calling. For a young woman to dream of wearing a uniform, implies to a wealthy and happy marriage.

URGENT

To dream that you are aiding the furtherance of an urgent appeal, predicts undertakings that may involve you and find great trouble in extricating yourself.

URN

To dream of urns, denotes that you will turn a struggling business into great account, greatly to the surprise of others. If they are broken; troubles in business.

USURPER

To dream that you are seizing, or holding property to which you have no legal right, denotes that you will have trouble over possessions, or in esstablishing a good credit. To dream that others are usurping your rights, implies keen competition in business that will put you to the test in learning how to win.

V

"When he was set down on the judgment seat, his wife sent unto him, saying, 'Have thou nothing to do with that just man; for I have suffered many things this day in my dream, because of him.,"— *Matthew* xxvii, 19.

VACCINATE

To dream of seeing others vaccinated, denotes that you are too easily lead by flattery and seldom think until it is too late. To dream of being vaccinated yourself, denotes that the finger of suspicion . will be pointed at you, of which you will experience some trouble in proving your innocence. For a woman to dream of being vaccinated on the leg, denotes false reports regarding her character.

VAGRANT

To dream of seeing vagrants, denotes a fright from a report of illness in the community. To help, or feed one; many happy returns. To dream that you are one; obstacles and annoyances to combat with.

VALENTINE

To dream of receiving a valentine, denotes disappointments relating to the heart. To send them, augurs that you will let good opportunities slip through your fingers.

VALISE

To dream of finding a valise, denotes an abundance. To lose one; sorrow and many struggles in reaching your goal.

VARNISH

To see others varnishing in your dream, augurs vexations through the interferences of others in your daily duties. To varnish yourself; your thrifty and economical qualties are highly appreciated by your superiors.

VASE

To dream of a beautiful vase, denotes many happy conditions to surround you in your future. To dream that you drop a vase and break it; shattered hopes, relating to business plans. For a woman to dream of receiving a vase as a gift, implies that her ambitions will be crowned with success.

VAULT

To dream of a vault containing money, signifies that your conduct and way of living perplexes many and puts them to thinking. To dream of a vault for the dead; sad tidings, and things to go wrong in general.

VEGETABLES

To dream that you are eating vegetables is an indication of ups and downs. You may think that you are on solid footing and all of a sudden things may give way from under you. These uncertainties are generally caused by those you sincerely trusted. To dream of decayed vegetables, denotes disappointments. To dream of preparing them for a meal, implies that success will come gradually but surely.

VEHICLE

To dream that you are thrown from a vehicle, augurs gossip that will irritate you and you will stop at nothing to sift it to the bottom. To ride in one successful and without any mishap, denotes triumph over resistance.

VEIL

To dream of a veil in general, denotes that you are not as sincere with friends as you might be. To dream of losing a veil, augurs a dispute with a man. To see in your dream a bridal veil, denotes a change that will be propitious. To dream of wearing a bridal veil, predicts an affair that will consummate successfully. To dream of mourning veils, augurs disappointments and troubles.

VEINS

To dream of seeing bleeding veins, denotes sorrows and troubles without an end.

VELVET

To dream of velvet is a happy augury, it omens much happiness to the dreamer. For an unmarried woman to dream that she is wearing a dress of velvet, denotes many suitors that will ask for her hand and heart.—Wealth will be her portion.

VENTRILOQUIST

To dream that you are a ventriloquist, denotes that people will put you down as shrewd and cunning and are afraid to have dealings with you. To dream of listening to a ventriloquist, denotes that you must guard your tongue more in society.

VERMIN

To dream of seeing vermin crawling about, augurs anxiety due to sickness. To dream that you succeed in exterminating it, denotes victory in an attempt.

VICE

To dream that you are encouraging vice in any form, denotes that you are in danger of losing your good name.

VICTIM

To dream that you are a victim of another's clever doings, denotes that others will seek to injure you. To dream that you victimize another, implies to wealth gained by unquestionable manners.

VICTORY

To dream that you are victorious in any contest, or feat, denotes that you will trip your enemies to their great surprise.

VINE

To dream of creeping vines, is a happy augury. If they contain blossoms, the sick will soon get well, and the well more rugged and robust. To dream of vines that are poisonous, augurs a rundown vitality that needs looking after.

VINEGAR

To dream of vinegar in general, denotes difficulties or obstacles of some kind. To dream of drinking it means worries and duties to perform that are anything but pleasant.

VINEYARD

To dream of being in a vineyard with all its lucious fruit, denotes joy as the result of successful ventures. To the lover it predicts an early marriage. To dream of one and its fruit out of season would not be so propitious.

VIOLETS

To dream of violets is a splendid sign. For an unmarried woman to gather them, denotes that she will soon meet her future fate, as regards a husband.

To dream that you gather them in abundance, augurs fame and riches.

VIOLIN

To dream of seeing some one play the violin and that the music is harmoniously sweet, denotes to the man of business that pending investments will turn into unexpected good fortune. For an unmarried woman to dream of a violin, her asperation will be crowned to the height of her ambition.

VIRGIN

To dream of a virgin is very propitious, it denotes success in many directions. For an unmarried woman to dream that she is no longer in this state, denotes that her love for frivolity and gaities will jeopardize her good name by becoming or acting too intimate with her male associates. To a married woman, that she is still a virgin, denotes that certain conditions will bring about her past that will produce remorse. For a man to dream of outraging one in an illicit manner predicts that his plans relating to business will be slow and unwarranting.

VISIT

To dream that you are visiting is a happy omen, more so if the visit has been pleasant and congenial. To dream that a friend visits you, omens good news from one whom you like. To dream of receiving a visit from one who appears in distress, would mean struggles and disappointment.

VISIONS

To have some one appear in a vision that you know, relates to troubles in your family. To dream of having strange and confused visions to confront you, denotes an illness.

VOICES

To hear voices in your dreams, that is if they are calm and not distressing, denotes pleasure and contentment. Should they be harsh or angry, disappointments are signaled to the dreamer. To hear weeping voices, is a warning to guard your tongue while in a fit of passion.

VOLCANO

To dream of a volcano in eruption, augurs differences that have to be adjusted. The dreamer should exercise much care after such a dream as to what he says to those he may have differences with.

VOMIT

To see others vomiting in your dream, denotes that you will be harassed by the false sayings of others. To dream that you are vomiting implies that there is danger of an illness for you.

VOTE

To dream of voting, denotes an appeal in your community on which your signature is solicited. To dream of being paid to vote a certain way, or for a certain party, augurs that you will take a step against your better judgment.

VOW

To dream that you see some one making a vow, denotes complaint, regarding the conducting of your affairs. To take, or make a vow yourself; deceit, delusion.

VULTURES

To dream of vultures generally refers to prolonged illnesses, sometimes to enemies that are trying to harm you.

W

"Dreams are prophetic and cast their shadows of coming events before."

WADING

To dream of wading in clear water, denotes joy and pleasure.

WAGER

To dream of betting, denotes that you are seeking to turn your plans by deceptive actions. To lose a wager implies wrongs committed at the hands of those that dislike you.

WAGES

To dream of receiving wages, augurs a change greatly to your advantage. To dream of an increase in wages; profitable undertakings. To have them reduced, unpleasant things from those you highly esteemed.

WAGON

To dream of a wagon, forebodes discontentment, an unsettled in general. To dream of getting into a wagon, augurs shame due to some slight mishap. To dream of getting out of one, loss and a possible struggle for your rights. To dream of riding down hill, a hope to be furthered. Up hill, an evidence of discouragement, relating to work. To drive over an embankment, implies to sorrow and bereavement. To dream that you are driving very close to the edge of a precipice, denotes some illicit entanglement over which you will be greatly vexed.

WAITER

To dream that a waiter is pleasantly attending to your wants, denotes happy hours spent in the presence of friends. To see one cross and disobliging, augurs that you will be bored by friends.

WALKING

To dream that you are walking and filled with energy, denotes consolation and happiness. To dream of walking and find difficulty in making headway, implies to troubles and pain. To walk in the night; struggles and complications.

WALLET

To dream of seeing a wallet filled with money, denotes good fortune. To see an old one and empty; many cares and struggles.

WALLS

To dream of coming across a wall and are unable to pass, denotes difficulties in convincing others to your way of thinking. To dream that you jump over one; you will be able to surmount all obstacles and reach your ambition. To dream that you are walking on top of a high wall with perfect ease, forebodes bright sailing in your business in the future.

WALNUT

To dream of these nuts is a happy augury. To dream of opening them, or eating them, means difficulties followed by wealth and satisfaction. To dream of gathering them; discovery of a treasure.

WANT

To dream of seeing others in want, implies to dissatisfaction in services rendered by others. To dream that you are in want, denotes that you are too thoughtless of the future, you should cultivate more accummulative power.

WAR

To see war going on in your dream, denotes friction in the domestic circle. To dream that you are in war, denotes persecution. For a young woman to dream that her sweetheart is going to war, augurs scandal relating to a near friend.

WARDROBE

To dream of having a large and splendid wardrobe, denotes profit and rapid strides to the front. To dream of having a poor wardrobe; you are displeased with your community and the people.

WARTS

To dream of seeing warts on your person, means an annoyance, or that you are unable to get out of a certain thing, or affair. To dream of seeing them on others, is a sign of enemies in your midst unbeknown to you.

WASHING

To dream of washing, denotes that some personal interest will suffer through misjudgment. To dream of washing your body or face augurs that you may have to pocket your pride to ask for a certain thing.

WASP

To dream of wasps, denotes enemies that are endeavoring to malign you. To dream that they sting you, you will be much vexed to learn the work that spiteful enemies have wrought.

WATCH

To dream that you break a watch, denotes that trouble is ahead of you. To see watches in your dream, relates to successful speculations. To dream of receiving a watch; pleasant recreations.

WATER

To dream of being in, or on troubled waters, denotes a disappointment, relating to a deal. To dream of crossing a muddy stream, augurs troubles in collecting money that is due you. To dream of throwing small stones into the water and the water is clear that you can see them sink to the bottom, denotes that you will receive something that you have been anxiously awaiting. To dream of seeing clear water is always good. Muddy water always forebodes gloom and discontment. To dream of seeing water rise so high that it comes into your house, denotes a great struggle in resisting an evil. To fall into water that is muddy, predicts that you will suffer from many mistakes. To drink water that is not clear, forebodes sickness. To drink clear water; health.

WATERFALL

To see in your dream a nice clear waterfall, denotes that your ambitions will be realized, and that you will live in affluence.

WAVES

To dream of seeing clear waves, denotes pleasure and the accumulation of much wisdom. To see them muddy and choppy; losses from lack of proper judgment.

WEALTH

To dream of wealth, or see others wealthy, denotes the sincerity of friends that would help you should you meet with reverses. To dream that you are very wealthy, predicts that your stamina and aggression will carry you to your goal. For an unmarried woman to dream that her associates are wealthy, implies that she has high ideals and that there is great possibility of having them realized.

WEAVING

To dream of weaving and all works smoothly; your painstaking efforts will bear much fruit. To meet with many mishaps while weaving, such as the entanglement of ends, or the breaking of the

loom; struggles and possible defeat in your undertaking. To see others weaving; favorable conditions will surround you.

WEDDING

To dream of a wedding, forebodes an early ap-
proach of discontent and bitterness. To dream that
you are wedded secretly; discovery of gossip attack-
ing your character. To dream that there are oppositions to your wedding denotes jealous rivals.

WEDDING CLOTHES

To see wedding clothes in your dream, denotes
that your duties will be pleasing and from the heart
and that you will meet new and interesting friends.

WEDDING RING

To dream of a wedding ring, denotes that life
has much in store that is pleasing, and that things
will travel in a circle with little to mar happiness.

WEDLOCK

For a woman to dream that she is unhappy in
wedlock, denotes that many disagreeable things will
assail her ears, and that others are addicted to watch
her affairs too closely. To dream of severing wedlock, denotes disappointment and grief and many
petty jealousies.

WEEPING

To dream that you are weeping, generally brings
about sad news, or upheavels in the domestic circle.
To dream of seeing others weep, denotes, hope, joy,
after much contention. To the unmarried, to
dream of weeping, omens troubles in love.

WET

To dream of being wet, often is a warning foɪ the dreamer to look well after his physical welfare, as exposure, while being over-heated may bring about an illness. For a woman to dream of being wet to the skin, augurs trouble and disgrace resulting from an illegal attachment.

WHALE

To dream of seeing a large whale bent on destruction, denotes struggles and possible loss of property.

WHEAT

To dream of seeing it in the ear; profit and wealth to the dreamer. To see it in large quantities; plenty of riches. To see large fields of wheat; encouraging prospects. To see it in sacks; ambition will be crowned. To see it in a granary, but diminishing gradually; enemies may work you harm.

WHEELS

To gaze upon rapid moving wheels in your dreams, denotes success in business and matters will adjust themselves in family affairs. To set broken wheels, relates to a disappointment.

WHIP

To dream of a whip or hear the cracking of a whip, augurs difficulties and many things that need attending to.

WHIRLPOOL

To see a whirlpool in your dream, predicts troubles in business and that much mental exertion will fall to the dreamer. If it be dirty; enemies may work mischief.

WHIRLWIND

To dream that you are caught in a whirlwind, denotes that a change is soon to be brought about that will not be in accordance with your taste.

WHISKEY

To dream of whiskey put up in any form, denotes that you will push your selfish propensities to such an extent that you will become disliked by your friends. To dream of drinking it; many struggles before you reach your desired goal. To see others drinking it; money gained through much scheming.

WHISTLE

To dream that you are whistling, denotes that you are looking forward to an event in which you will figure conspicuously and where others will criticise you unjustly. To hear others whistle, predicts that you will be outrivaled in a prospective plan, by friends who mean to joke.

WIDOW

To dream of being a widow, denotes troubles and many vexing things to be said by others. For a man to dream that he marries a widow, augurs shattered hopes and thwarted ambition.

WIFE

To see your wife in your dream, denotes domestic troubles, generally due to the magnified suspicion on the part of the wife. To dream that your wife is lovable and agreeable; success, good business. To dream of fighting with your wife, or beating her; there is cause for the wife's suspicion. For a husband to dream that his wife is in the embrace of another; disappointing business proposition.

WIG

To dream that you are compelled to wear a wig, on account of loss of hair; predicts that you will be induced to make a change that you will regret. To see others wearing them; ill is being wished you.

WILD

To dream that you are turning wild, augurs misfortune through some careless act. To see others in this state; mental disturbance and conditions hard to account for.

WILL

To dream that you are making your will, denotes melancholy, trials, an unhappy mind. To dream that a will is made in someone else's favor instead of yours; disputes and quarrels of a shameful nature. To dream that you made a will and then destroyed it again, predicts that there is trouble abrewing that will soon come to light.

WIND

To dream that you hear the wind blowing loud and furious, predicts agony and torment at the hand of competitors. To dream that wind is blowing you back and resists your efforts; disappointment relating to some cherished hope.

WIND MILL

To dream of seeing a wind mill, denotes an abundance and that you will reach honor and position and be an influential light in your community.

WINDOW

To dream of open windows; intrigues under your very nose. To see them closed; you will be denied that which you crave for. To dream of jumping through a window, predicts trouble near at hand. To dream of stealing through a window, a possibility of a lawsuit.

WINGS

To dream that you have wings and are able to fly, denotes that you take and shoulder the troubles of others too much, consequently you fret and stew without a cause.

WINTER

To dream of winter when in reality that season is not here, omens a slight loss to the dreamer. generally brought about through illness.

WIRE

To dream of being caught, or entangled in a wire. denotes that you are feared as your disposition is so stern that others are afraid of you. To see rusty wire in your dream, denotes troubles due to an uncontrollable temper.

WITCH

To dream of these mysterious wonder workers denotes a lull in business greatly to your dissatisfaction, and that you are seeking avenues to better your conditions which will be slow in materializing.

WIZARD

To see in your dream an individual who claims to work wonders, denotes that you will be annoyed not only in business, but in public affairs as well.

WOLF

To dream that wolves are following you while driving, but are unable to harm you, signifies success in business. To dream that you kill one, foretells that those whom you trust will deceive you, by failing to make good that which they promised. To see a pack of wolves; you love to win through sharp scheming.

WOMAN

To dream that you quarrel or slap a woman denotes a disappointment with one whom you are intensely desirous of meeting. To dream of seeing a woman hiding, signifies that some unscrupulous person is palming himself off on your reputation. To dream that some woman is watching you, denotes that a former misunderstanding will be righted and all will be well again. To dream of kissing (for a man) a woman illicitly, or perhaps commit adultery omens bad. You will have much trouble from a woman, you were once intimate with. To see a pregnant one, augurs agreeable news. To see one with a beautiful figure; joy, satisfaction, if the dreamer be a man. To a woman this would mean jealousy, quarrel and scandal. To dream of seeing a woman quarrel; disappointment.

WOOL

To dream of seeing wool, augurs slow but sure prosperity and that you will grow to be a leading light in your community. Should the wool be in such a condition that it cannot be used, forebodes differences that will not coincide with others and you will be stimatized as stubborn.

WORK

To dream of seeing others at work, denotes money gained after a good deal of hard work and care. To dream that you are at work yourself, denotes success after having tried many different things, for past experiences have forced the mind into truer conditions.

WORMS

To dream of seeing worms on or near your body, denotes little ambition and that the dreamer lacks selfreliance and becomes too easily discouraged. To dream of killing them, predicts that you will determine to built character in this direction. To use them for fishing purposes, you will make some sudden gain greatly to the surprise of friends.

WOUND

To dream of seeing others wounded, predicts an injury, or wrong at the hands of those you thought were good friends. To have a wound yourself, augurs business troubles and many things to annoy you.

WRECKS

To dream of seeing a wreck, denotes many hard and distressing pulls in business and that you may seek another calling.

WREATH

To dream of a wreath that is fresh and pretty; gains, prosperity. To see one that is withered, predicts illness, or unhappiness from the hands of loved ones.

WRITING

To dream that you see others write denotes accusations from those you tried to please. To write yourself, denotes a blunder of the head that will probably cause a loss in business. To read writing; watch those that are trying to interest you in new schemes.

Y

"God came to Laban, the Syrian, by night, in a dream, and said unto him, take heed that thou speak not to Jacob, either good or bad."—*Gen.* xxxi., 24.

YACHT

To dream of seeing a yacht, denotes optimism and foresight and that your efforts are strengthened, or reinforced with recreation. To see one in distress, denotes that business compels you to disappoint friends who are on pleasure bent.

YARD STICK

To see or use a yard stick in your dream, denotes that your exacting ways are disliked by others and on this account are often shunned.

YARN

To dream that you are working with yarn and experience difficulty in undoing it, predicts slight vexations due to disappointments. To handle it successfully; success in whatever you may attempt. For a young woman to dream of yarn, denotes that she is looked upon with high esteem by her lover.

YAWNING

To dream of seeing others yawn, augurs unpleasant conditions and even illness to the dreamer. To yawn yourself, denotes that you are restless, nervous and never satisfied with your fate.

Z

"Therefore night shall be unto you, that ye shall not have a vision, and it shall be dark unto you, that ye shall not divine; and the sun shall go down over the prophets, and the day shall be dark over them."—*Mich.* iii., 6.

ZEBRA

To dream of seeing a herd of zebras, denotes that you are wasting time and energy on an enterprise that will bring you no good. To dream you see one that is tame, or that you pet one, denotes returns from a source that will be much to your delight and satisfaction.

ZEPHYR

To dream of zephyrs, if they be soft relates to sentiment. You will sacrifice much for the one you love and let sentiment interfere with business. For an unmarried woman to dream that she is gloomed by zephyrs soft touch, denotes petty inquietude, inconstancy, etc.

ZINC

To dream of zinc omens good luck to the dreamer. Business will soon climb to a paying basis that the dreamer may enjoy many luxuries.

ZODIAC

To dream of seeing or studying the system of the zodiacs, predicts fame and riches to the dreamer through his love for wisdom and loyal benevolency to humanity.